Quality of Care in
Residential Homes for the Elderly

Quality of Care in Residential Homes for the Elderly

Dr Dennis Green

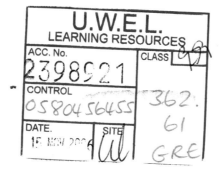

BSi

Business
Information

Dedication

This book is dedicated:

to my wife, Margaret

to three daughters and three sons-in-law

Alison and John

Helen and Anthony

Caroline and Karl

and to eight grandchildren

Thomas, Lucy, Sophie and Emily

Harriet and Alexander

Jessica and Rebecca

BSI reference: BIP 2072

ISBN 0 580 45645 5

Typeset by Typobatics Ltd

Printed by MPG Books Ltd, Bodmin, Cornwall

Table of Contents

Appendix 2: References

Preface

The idea of writing a book on the application of the ISO 9001:2000 quality management standard to care homes for the elderly arose shortly after I had audited such a home, whilst being monitored by someone from the United Kingdom Accreditation Service (UKAS) and someone from the Education Department of the Social Care Association. I had done an enormous amount of preparatory work for the certification audit. As lead auditor, when I chaired the closing meeting I recommended that the home should be awarded a certificate and the home subsequently received it.

I had carefully documented all the work that I had done in my own time before the audit. These documents were based on the study of several key documents: The Care Homes Regulations 2001, including a number of schedules, Care Homes for Older People: National Minimum Standards and The Management of Medication in Care Services.

When I integrated the key aspects of these documents with what I knew about the requirements of ISO 9001, I had produced a large set of notes. All this work was necessary because one of the requirements of ISO 9001 is that all regulatory and statutory requirements have to be addressed satisfactorily. At end of the day I was satisfied that the home did, in fact, from the objective evidence that I found, satisfy all such requirements and the requirements of the ISO 9001.

My experience convinced me that I should write this book, especially since no one, as far as I knew, had written on this important subject.

Chapter 1 provides background reading that is essential to set the scene, including the relevant regulatory and statutory documents. Chapter 2 classifies the different kinds of documents that a home might decide to use. A few are mandatory, such as the quality policy, but otherwise the home can decide what documentation it needs to run the home efficiently in the best interests of the residents in which quality of care is paramount. It is advisable to classify documents. One way is suggested by the examples given in Chapter 2, but the home can choose whatever way seems best.

Chapter 3 is devoted to process diagrams. Process diagrams are explained and several flow diagrams are included as examples. Note that process diagram PD 102 (Figures 3.4 and 3.5) is in the form of a traditional diagram whereas PD 104 (Figure 3.7) is a more modern diagram produced by more sophisticated computer software. The home is free to decide which method to use.

Chapters 4 to 8 address the requirements of the corresponding clauses of ISO 9001.

Chapter 7, Product realization, comments on requirements that relate to applicable regulations, schedules and standards associated with care homes. These have been identified for the reader in the relevant places.

Chapter 7 is exceptional in that parts of it need not be addressed, provided any exclusions can be justified and the exclusions are explained in the quality manual.

Chapter 9 is devoted to guideline audit questions. Questions that are particularly relevant to regulations and standards are printed in italics.

Appendix 1 includes the six mandatory procedures required by ISO 9001. These are: control of documents; control of records; internal audit; control of nonconforming product; corrective action; and preventive action.

The book also includes a typical quality policy that addresses the requirements of ISO 9001, a statement of possible quality objectives and a suggested organization chart. Appendix 2 gives a list of references.

This book should be of special interest to many people who have responsibility for the care of elderly people in residential care homes and who want to maintain and, whenever possible, improve the quality of life of the residents through a quality management system based on the international standard ISO 9001.

It is hoped that this book will benefit many different kinds of manager. First I hope that it will be of interest to what the standards refer to as top management. These are people who direct and control organizations. For the first time an external auditor from a certification body is expected to make a judgement on whether there is a commitment by top management to its quality management system. A committed top manager is more likely to create a new culture in which corporate competence and individual competence are at the forefront of all levels of management and the workforce.

The book should also be of interest to quality professionals as well as to those who aspire to become one. This includes internal auditors and third-party auditors.

The views expressed are those of the author. The author is confident that if the guidelines included in this book are followed, in interpreting the five requirement clauses of ISO 9001 and the regulations and standards applicable to residential care homes, the home is likely to achieve accredited certification to ISO 9001 at the first attempt. Perhaps what is much more important is that the quality of care of all the elderly residents in such a home will thereby be enhanced.

It would be impossible to thank personally all those who have made this book possible. Much of the book is based on my experience as an auditor, mainly auditing against the quality management standards on behalf of certification bodies. I should like to express my thanks to these certification bodies, which have provided me with many opportunities for third-party auditing. I should also like to thank the people in many organizations whom I have subjected to the rigours of third-party auditing. All the people that I have met at different levels within such organizations have, without exception, received me kindly into their organizations to enable me to carry out my duties. Without such acceptance, auditing would have become an unwelcome task and one that I would have abandoned a long time ago.

Chapter 1:
General introduction

The age distribution of the UK's population has been changing over the last few decades. This is partly because people are having fewer children. The other reason is that modern medicine and surgery are now based on scientific and technological developments that enable doctors to treat patients in ways that were inconceivable a few decades ago. As a result, many patients with what used to be life-threatening diseases or conditions recover and live much longer than they did previously.

Amongst the ever increasing number of elderly people, whether they have been in hospital or not, there are some who need support for day-to-day living in their own homes. This is particularly the case when there is no longer a partner to act as carer. This situation is aggravated when children of the elderly people are unable to give much day-to-day support because they have other responsibilities, however much they would like to. It is because some elderly people need to be cared for in their homes that a caring services industry has been developed over the last few years in which home carers now visit elderly people in their homes on a regular planned basis to give them personal care and domestic help. Many thousands of elderly people now receive help in their own homes. Some hundreds of domiciliary home care organizations have been established to provide such care.

Elderly people need additional nursing care that used to be provided in hospital. It is because of the increasing demands being made on the National Health Service hospitals for the diagnosis and treatment of illnesses that long term nursing of elderly people in our hospitals is no longer an option. As a result there are now many nursing care homes or 'care home, N' (N standing for nursing) throughout the country for elderly people, where residential care with appropriate nursing is provided.

There are other new types of classification for care homes, e.g. DE means that the care home specializes in dementia care; MD stands for mental disorder; PD for physical disabilities.

There is another possible provision for elderly people: the residential care home, or 'care home, PC' (PC standing for personal care). Such homes provide all the basic needs of elderly people whose nursing needs are minimal, in a safe and caring environment. In these homes, whenever a nursing or medical need arises then such needs are provided by external resources, such as community care nurses and general practitioners.

According to a recent National Care Standards Commission (NCSC) report [1], there are 22,836 social care establishments registered on their database. These include care homes for elderly people; care homes for younger adults; and children's homes. A recent *Which?* report [2] states that the Office of Fair Trading has been persuaded to investigate the £9 billion pounds a year care homes market.

Statutory requirements

Following the Care Standards Act, 2000, the National Care Standards Commission (NCSC) was established. On 1 April 2004, this commission was replaced by the Commission for Social Care and Inspection (CSCI). This new inspectorate brings together the social care functions of the former NCSC; the work previously undertaken by the Social Services Inspectorate; the joint Review Team of the Social Services Inspectorate; and the work of the Audit Commission.

All care homes must abide by the *Care Homes Regulations* published in 2001 by the former NCSC [3]. These regulations came into force on 1 April 2002. The Regulations are mandatory. There are 46 regulations supplemented by seven schedules.

In February 2003, the Department of Health published the third edition of the *Care Homes for Older People: National Minimum Standards* [4]. It became effective on 1 June 2003. There are 38 national minimum standards:

Standards 1–6	Choice of home;
Standards 7–11	Health and personal care;
Standards 12–15	Daily life and social activities;
Standards 16–8	Complaints and protection;
Standards 19–26	Environment;
Standards 27–30	Staffing;
Standards 31–38	Management and administration.

These standards have no statutory powers, but are similar to codes of practice. The failure to address some or all of the national minimum standards is not likely to go unnoticed by inspectors. Compliance with such codes is a positive factor when members of the inspectorate are determining whether a residential home meets the needs, and secures the welfare and social inclusion of the people who live in such homes. However, failure to comply with these standards might result in a residential care home being de-registered.

All registered care homes undergo external twice-yearly inspections. The weakness of this system of inspections is that there is no requirement for formalized on-going systematic internal auditing to be carried out by the staff of such homes, as is the case with ISO 9001.

ISO 9001 quality management systems

ISO 9001 is not about perfection. It is about striving at all times to do a first-class job, as specified, while at the same time seeking to make improvements. This applies to all staff. In fact, there is an overall requirement in the standard to continually improve the effectiveness of the quality management system. As a quality management system is gradually introduced, this ethos should permeate all aspects of the activities in a home.

The standard requires the establishment of a quality management system. Top management must be committed to the quality management system. It must also be committed to satisfying the needs and expectations of its customers – in this case, residents – to ensure that the quality of care received by all residents is beyond reproach. It must ensure that the activities of the home are well planned; that responsibilities and authorities are defined and made known to all employees; and that lines of communication are in place and known by all employees. A management representative must be appointed. They are usually named as the quality manager who has responsibility on a day-to-day basis for ensuring the smooth running of the quality management system. Top management must conduct management reviews on a regular planned basis.

One criticism of the precursor of ISO 9001: 2000, i.e. the 1994 standard, was that it was not suitable for organizations that employ only a small number of people. This is a charge that cannot be made against the revised standard. The documentation requirements are minimal. The focus is on processes and flow or process diagrams with minimum documentation (as decided by the organization itself) to plan, operate and control the processes. A quality policy statement is required. Measurable quality objectives, several or many, have to be set, as decided by the organization. Only six procedures are mandatory. A quality manual is required; the size of the manual can be decided by the organization. All such documentation integrates all aspects of the residential home's quality management system, which is focused on the quality of care provided for the residents in the home.

Internal auditing is a very important requirement of the international standard. Internal auditors must be trained to seek out objective evidence and ensure that mistakes and omissions are recorded in a systematic manner, and then corrected and followed through to a satisfactory conclusion [5].

There is an important and significant word in the revised standard: 'competence'. Some carers in a residential care home have few, if any, qualifications, but this does not mean that these carers cannot be trained to do a good and useful job in a residential home. They must undergo appropriate training so that they are competent to do the tasks allocated to them. If competence testing shows that after training they are still incompetent, further training must be offered. Competence is a 'yes' or 'no' issue: there is no halfway house. Being competent in the business of caring for elderly people is of paramount importance: if carers fail to do what is expected of them, then elderly people in the home suffer unnecessarily and the quality of care becomes unacceptable. Thus, training, competence testing and evaluation of training are all very important and they are key to the success of any residential care home. By April 2005, 50% of all staff working in any care home for the elderly must have at least an NVQ level 2 qualification in care.

There are many other requirements in the standard that apply to care homes. These include requirements to:

- plan and control all the services provided;

- monitor all the processes associated with the organization's services;

- monitor the satisfaction of those being cared for;

- deal with the complaints received from those being cared for;

- take timely corrective action when things go wrong;

- take preventive action when a possible problem is envisaged,

- prevent an adverse event from happening in the first place;

- analyse data collected; and

- have the required documentation in place.

Good organizations already fulfil many of the ISO 9001 requirements. Others will find that preparing for certification to ISO 9001 will help them to become more efficient. Nothing in the standard is intended to be bureaucratic. In many cases an organization can decide for itself how to satisfy a particular requirement of the standard. For instance, an organization can determine for itself how it monitors (not measures) customer satisfaction. In due course, an external auditor will make an assessment from the objective evidence found and decide, on behalf of the chosen certification body, whether the requirements of the standard have been met.

Once an organization has decided to seek certification to ISO 9001, the improvements in the organization start to become self-evident to management, to employees and, in due course, to the residents themselves. Moreover, when employees know that top management really is striving to get things right and to do things better, all the time, they become proud to be part of such an organization and soon become keen to suggest improvements.

Organizations seeking certification against the requirements of ISO 9001 are audited by professionally qualified auditors. Such auditors are commissioned by certification bodies, which in turn are scrutinized by national bodies. In the UK this body is the United Kingdom Accreditation Service (UKAS). UKAS itself is scrutinized by an external organization to ensure that it too is complying with international agreements for such bodies. Thus, every effort is made to ensure that any accredited certifications are worthy of the name and are awarded against the same international criteria.

The climax to such preparation is the award of a certificate, but it does not stop at that point. It is just the beginning of an on-going process of 'continual improvement in the effectiveness of the quality management system' with associated improvements in the quality of care being provided for elderly people in the residential home. The independent certification body that awarded the certificate will continue to visit the organization, usually twice each year, to ensure that the organization continues to satisfy the requirements of the standard and, most importantly, that it continues to improve the effectiveness of the quality management system and thereby maintains and possibly improves the quality of care for residents in the home. Such visits will focus in particular on the continuing requirement to satisfy the needs and expectations of the elderly people in their home, by provision of quality care for each resident, as well as checking that any recent new regulations or legislation have been addressed satisfactorily.

The latest international survey on ISO 9001 shows that over half a million organizations worldwide have been awarded a certificate for compliance with the requirements of the quality management systems standard [6]. This is a clear indication of its effectiveness.

Residential care homes and the quality management systems standard

One of the important requirements of ISO 9001 is that all statutory and regulatory requirements are met [see ISO 9001, clause 7.2.1(c)]. This means that before a certificate can be awarded by a certification body all the statutory and regulatory requirements specified in section 2 must be addressed.

The product and services of a residential care home

ISO 9001 refers throughout to 'product'. It states that this is to be interpreted as product or service, or both.

There is a need to clarify what is meant by the product of a residential home. I have defined it as the 'maintenance and possible improvement of the quality of life' of the residents. It is a somewhat cumbersome definition, but it helps with the interpretation of the standard when applied to residential homes.

There is no doubt about what is meant by 'services' in the context of a residential home. The services provided are all the caring and other activities that are provided for the benefit of residents, whether they are direct or indirect benefits.

Quality assurance

The staff in the residential home also needs to understand the significance of quality assurance. I have defined 'quality assurance' as follows:

> Quality assurance is a pledge to a customer/resident that the quality (as seen, demonstrated, defined, agreed and accepted) will be maintained for a particular product (e.g. food) or a particular service (e.g. cleanliness).

The way forward

If carers and other staff work closely with top management (within a framework of a quality management system based on ISO 9001) and if everyone works in an atmosphere of 'openness, integrity and responsibility' there is no reason why British residential homes cannot become the envy of the world. This book is intended to give guidance to all those working in residential homes who aspire to contributing to providing quality residential care through ISO 9001 quality management systems.

Chapter 2:
Residential care home documentation

Documentation is a generic term that includes all the documents, records and data used in a residential home. In this chapter an attempt is made to clarify precisely what is meant by documentation. The introduction of ISO 9001 into a residential home might provide an opportunity for some rationalization of the existing documents.

Some homes may be in the process of computerizing all their documentation. This is to be encouraged, but the advice given in this chapter will stand whether this is the case or not.

Policy documents

A policy document in a home is one issued by or on behalf of top management. A policy document applies throughout the home to all staff in the home. A few examples of policy documents are:

> quality policy;
> quality objectives;
> the organization chart;
>
> confidentiality within the home;
> communications with outside bodies such as the press and media;
> access to personal records;
>
> sickness and absence;
> maternity leave;
>
> standards of dress;
>
> disciplinary issues;
> appeals;
> grievances.

Policy documents can be given the prefix PL and a number. Any new documents created in connection with the new quality management system may be identified by using numbers from 101 upwards whereas existing documents may be able to retain their numbers. See Table 2.1 for an example list of forms.

Table 2.1 – An example list of forms

FM 101	Control of Framework Documentation
FM 102	Acceptance of Documentation
FM 103	Register of Framework Documentation
FM 104	Framework Documentation – Change Request
FM 105	Changes to Framework Documentation
FM 121	Internal Audit Schedule
FM 122	Register of Internal Audits
FM 123	Internal Audit Questionnaire
FM 124	Nonconformity or Observation Form
FM 125	Summary – Internal Audit Report
FM 131	Register of Nonconformities
FM 132	Nonconformity Form
FM 141	Register of Complaints
FM 142	Complaint Form

Three very important policy documents are referred to in Chapter 5:

quality policy, PL 101

quality objectives, PL 102 and

the organization chart, PL 103.

When any existing policy documents are revised they should be re-numbered from 101 upwards if a new numbering system has been introduced as a result of preparation for ISO 9001 certification.

Processes and process diagrams

All homes will have one or more processes and some might already have process diagrams (PDs) in place (see Chapter 3).

Procedures

A procedure explains how things are carried out. Procedures give sufficient detail only for the staff for whom they are written. They are often supplementary to process diagrams and give details that cannot be stated on process diagrams. Procedures are identified by the code PC followed by a unique number. As will be clarified later, procedures PC 101–106 are mandatory procedures that are required for compliance with ISO 9001. There may be other procedures that a registered person might decide are required to ensure that the regulations or national minimum standards are addressed.

Work instructions

Work instructions give step-by-step instructions on how a specific task must be performed. No deviations are allowed without the specific authority of a senior member of staff, who thereby accepts full responsibility for any such deviations. Work instructions are indicated by the code WI followed by a unique number.

Forms

Residential homes use a number of forms. Forms are indicated by the code FM followed by a unique number.

External documents

External documents can be listed in a similar way to external forms. They are indicated by ED and are listed serially, for example:

Department of Health, ED 101, ED 102, etc.
Local Authority, ED 201, ED 202, etc.
Documents from professional bodies, ED 301, ED 302, etc.

External forms

If external forms are used or have to be completed by a home, each will have a unique number. It is not necessary for the home to give these forms additional numbers. External forms should simply be listed in whatever ways that the home decides are convenient. Groups of numbers might be allocated for different kinds of form.

External forms are indicated by EFM and are listed serially, for example:

Department of Health, EFM 101, EFM 102, etc.
Local Authority, EFM 201, EFM 202, etc.
Professional bodies, EFM 301, EFM 302, etc.

Home records

Documents such as home records provide objective evidence about residents within the home. Home records will include:

*   resident's care records;

*   care plans;

*   nursing care records;

*   medication records.

Quality management systems documentation

When a home decides to seek certification to the international quality management system standard ISO 9001, additional documentation and records need to be created in order to control the quality management system. These are explained in Chapter 4. Suffice it to say here that these are intended to be few in number. They are considered important for the quality management system and should enable management, carers and other staff to work closely together with the objective of maintaining and, whenever possible, improving the quality of life for all residents.

Chapter 3:
Process diagrams

A process is simply a series of activities that are carefully planned and executed to achieve the desired objectives. Any process is initiated through some form of input and the activities that follow will result in some form of output. In its simplest form a process will consist of:

- an input;

- one activity that adds value to the input; and

- a resulting output.

This is depicted in Figure 3.1.

In practice, many processes consist of a series of activities, each activity following on directly to the next activity, each of which adds further value, ultimately resulting in the required output. Such a series of carefully planned activities constitute a more typical process (see Figure 3.2).

All organizations have at least one core process; that is why an organization exists. Some organizations have several core processes. These are sometimes referred to as major processes or first-level processes. In this book they are referred to as first-level processes.

Process diagrams for a residential care home

Process diagrams can be used to advantage in a residential care home. Process diagram PD 101 (Figure 3.3) shows one example. This process diagram gives an overview of the steps to be taken by a home from the time that it receives an enquiry about the home to the time that a resident moves into the home, or alternatively, decides not to do so. The home might also conclude that the needs of a potential resident cannot be met so that no place can be offered in the home. The column on the left of PD 101 shows the person or persons responsible for ensuring that this process is adhered to when a resident is seeking a place in a home. The ultimate goal of this process is to ensure that if an enquirer does move into a home then the new resident will at least maintain their quality of life and, whenever possible, improve their quality of life.

Sometimes it is convenient to give each stage a number for easy reference when discussing a process. In PD 101 the stages have been numbered from 1 to 14.

Other process diagrams included in this book include:

PD 102   care plans (Figures 3.4 and 3.5);

PD 103   medication (Figure 3.6) [7];

PD 104   residents' complaints (Figure 3.7).

The management of each home can decide how many process diagrams are required.

Notes attached to processes

It is not always desirable or possible to show all the relevant information concerning a first-level process in one process diagram. One method to overcome this problem is to attach a note to a particular stage in a process diagram. In PD 101, a note has been attached to stage no. 2 (this is indicated by the letter 'N'). In this example, the note includes the details that are to be addressed in the home's statement of purpose and in the resident's guide. The note includes too much information to be included in a process diagram.

Lower-level processes

Another method of improving the content of a first-level process diagram is to add a lower-level diagram, i.e. a level 2 process diagram. This is demonstrated in process diagram 102 (see Figures 3.4 and 3.5). Note that in this case, stage no. 1 has a grey shadow on two of its sides. This indicates that there is a level 2 process associated with this stage.

Lower levels can be attached to any of the stages in a process diagram.

Advantages of process diagrams

The preparation of process diagrams can help homes to rationalize their major processes with the minimum amount of textual documentation. The attachment of notes to stages can be very useful and second-level diagrams enable more information to be displayed when and as required without making the first-level diagram too complicated. The process diagrams can be extended to yet further levels, which might contain important information that may not be relevant to many of the people working in accordance with the upper-level process diagrams. For instance, a first-level diagram might be very relevant to what a carer does each day for the residents, but most of the carers do not need to know about a lower-level diagram, which, for example, deals with checking of weighing scales or checking of refrigerator thermometers. All staff should have access to the process diagrams according to their need.

Bureaucracy

All processes can be depicted in process diagrams, a number of which are shown at the end of this chapter. Process diagrams are relatively easy to understand. They encourage all staff to focus on the all important output.

None of this is bureaucratic. Flow diagrams and the collection of information and data of the right kind, particularly using computers, provide a simple means of obtaining facts and findings so that top management can manage effectively in the interests of everyone, but especially of the residents.

Collection and analysis of such data is also a requirement of ISO 9001 with a view to putting top management in control and giving opportunities for top management continually to improve the effectiveness of its quality management system (see Chapter 8).

Figure 3.1 – A simple process

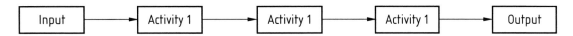

Figure 3.2 – A process showing consecutive activities

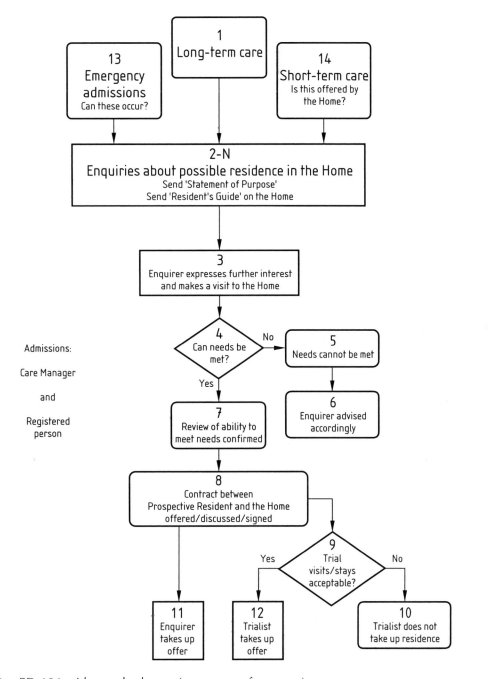

Figure 3.3 – PD 101 with attached note (statement of purpose)

Statement of purpose (Note to PD 101)

The statement of purpose must include the following:
Regulation 4(1)

(a)   a statement of the aims and objectives of the care home;

(b)   a statement as to the facilities and services that are to be provided by the registered provider or registered manager;

(c)   a statement as to the matters listed in Schedule 1 below.

Schedule 1

1.   the name and address of the registered provider and of any registered manager;

2.   the relevant qualifications and experience of the registered provider and any registered manager;

3.   the number, relevant qualifications and experience of the staff working at the care home;

4.   the organizational structure of the home;

5.   the age range and sex of the service users for whom the accommodation is intended;

6.   the range of needs that the care home is intended to meet;

7.   whether nursing is to be provided;

8.   any criteria used for admission to the care home, including the care home's policy and procedures (if any) for emergency admissions;

9.   the arrangements for residents to engage in social activities, hobbies and leisure interests;

10.   the arrangements made for consultation with residents about the operation of the care home;

11.   the fire precautions and associated emergency procedures in the care home;

12.   the arrangements made for residents to attend religious services of their choice;

13.   the arrangements made for contact between residents and their relatives, friends and representatives;

14.   the arrangements made for dealing with complaints;

15.   the arrangements made for dealing with reviews of the resident's care plan (Regulation 15(1));

16.   the number and size of rooms in the care home;

17.   details of any specific therapeutic techniques used in the care home and arrangements made for their supervision;

18.   the arrangements made for respecting the privacy and dignity of residents.

The service user's guide sent to a prospective resident must include the following: Regulation 5(1)

(a)   a summary of the statement of purpose;

(b)   the terms and conditions in respect of accommodation to be provided for residents, including the amount of payment and method of payment of fees;

(c)   a standard form of contract for the provision of services and facilities by the registered provider to residents;

(d)   a copy of the most recent inspection report;

(e)   a summary of the complaints procedure established under Regulation 22;

(f)   the address and telephone number of the Commission for Social Care and Inspection.

Standard 1.2

1.   a brief description of the services provided;

2.   a description of the individual accommodation and communal space provided;

3.   relevant qualifications and experience of the registered provider, manager and staff;

4.   the number of places provided and any special needs or interests catered for;

5.   a copy of the most recent inspection report;

6.   a copy of the complaints procedure;

7.   residents' views of the home.

(Note: There is clearly a need to rationalize some of the above statements.)

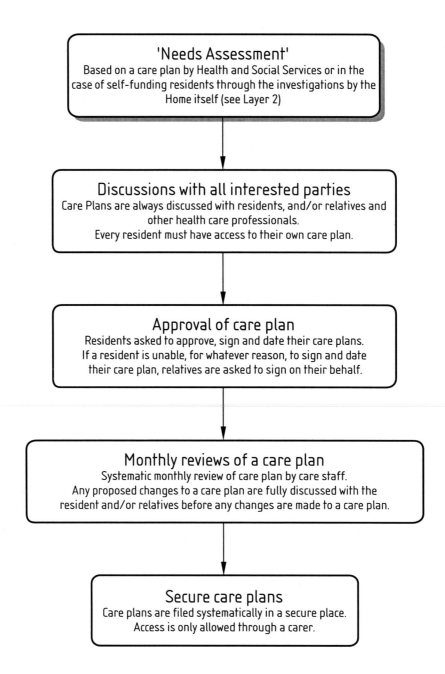

'Needs Assessment'
Based on a care plan by Health and Social Services or in the
case of self-funding residents through the investigations by the
Home itself (see Layer 2)

Discussions with all interested parties
Care Plans are always discussed with residents, and/or relatives and
other health care professionals.
Every resident must have access to their own care plan.

Approval of care plan
Residents asked to approve, sign and date their care plans.
If a resident is unable, for whatever reason, to sign and date
their care plan, relatives are asked to sign on their behalf.

Monthly reviews of a care plan
Systematic monthly review of care plan by care staff.
Any proposed changes to a care plan are fully discussed with the
resident and/or relatives before any changes are made to a care plan.

Secure care plans
Care plans are filed systematically in a secure place.
Access is only allowed through a carer.

Figure 3.4 – Care plan diagram 1 (PD 102)

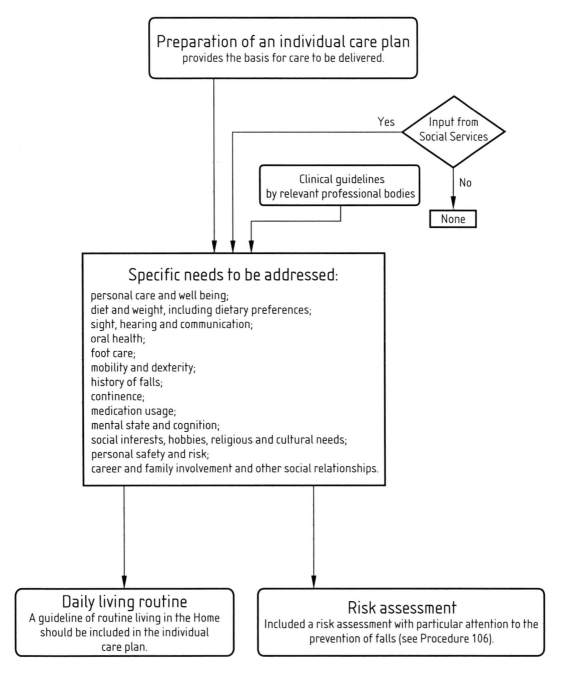

Figure 3.5 – Care plan diagram 2 (PD 102)

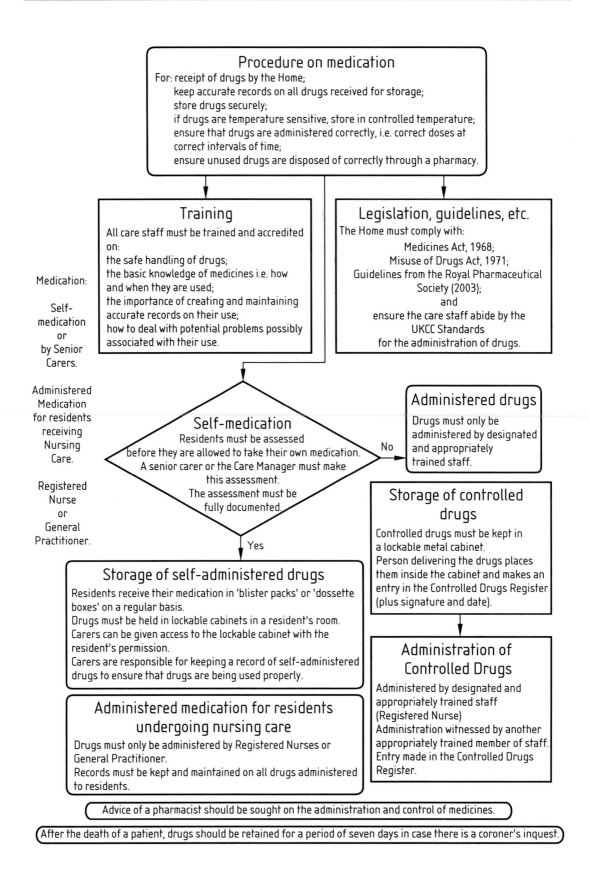

Procedure on medication
For: receipt of drugs by the Home;
        keep accurate records on all drugs received for storage;
        store drugs securely;
        if drugs are temperature sensitive, store in controlled temperature;
        ensure that drugs are administered correctly, i.e. correct doses at
        correct intervals of time;
        ensure unused drugs are disposed of correctly through a pharmacy.

Training
All care staff must be trained and accredited on:
the safe handling of drugs;
the basic knowledge of medicines i.e. how and when they are used;
the importance of creating and maintaining accurate records on their use;
how to deal with potential problems possibly associated with their use.

Legislation, guidelines, etc.
The Home must comply with:
Medicines Act, 1968;
Misuse of Drugs Act, 1971;
Guidelines from the Royal Pharmaceutical Society (2003);
and
ensure the care staff abide by the UKCC Standards
for the administration of drugs.

Medication:

Self-medication
or
by Senior Carers.

Administered Medication for residents receiving Nursing Care.

Registered Nurse
or
General Practitioner.

Self-medication
Residents must be assessed before they are allowed to take their own medication.
A senior carer or the Care Manager must make this assessment.
The assessment must be fully documented.

No

Yes

Administered drugs
Drugs must only be administered by designated and appropriately trained staff.

Storage of controlled drugs
Controlled drugs must be kept in a lockable metal cabinet.
Person delivering the drugs places them inside the cabinet and makes an entry in the Controlled Drugs Register (plus signature and date).

Storage of self-administered drugs
Residents receive their medication in 'blister packs' or 'dossette boxes' on a regular basis.
Drugs must be held in lockable cabinets in a resident's room.
Carers can be given access to the lockable cabinet with the resident's permission.
Carers are responsible for keeping a record of self-administered drugs to ensure that drugs are being used properly.

Administration of Controlled Drugs
Administered by designated and appropriately trained staff
(Registered Nurse)
Administration witnessed by another appropriately trained member of staff.
Entry made in the Controlled Drugs Register.

Administered medication for residents undergoing nursing care
Drugs must only be administered by Registered Nurses or General Practitioner.
Records must be kept and maintained on all drugs administered to residents.

Advice of a pharmacist should be sought on the administration and control of medicines.

After the death of a patient, drugs should be retained for a period of seven days in case there is a coroner's inquest.

Figure 3.6 – Procedure on medication (PD 103)

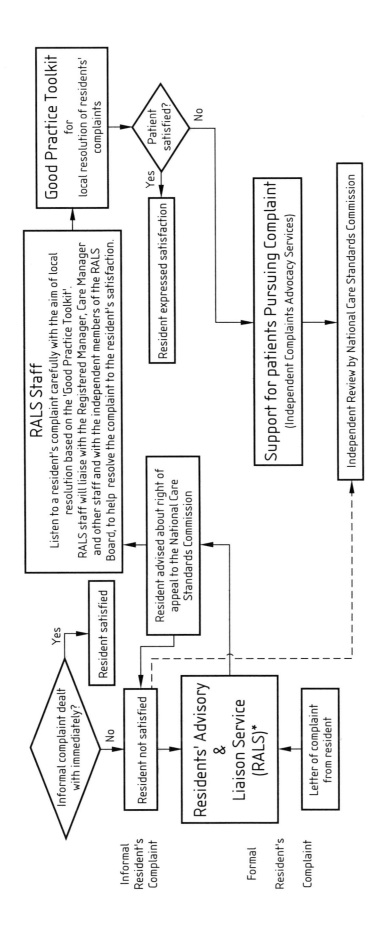

Figure 3.7 – Residents' complaints (PD 104)

Chapter 4:
Quality management system (Clause 4)

General requirements (ISO 9001, clause 4.1)

Any residential care home preparing for accredited certification to ISO 9001 must establish, document, implement and maintain a quality management system. Once a home has addressed the documentation requirements of the standard, the extent of the quality management system documentation can be decided by the home, depending on:

- the type of home;

- the size of the home;

- the complexity and interaction of the processes associated with the home;

- the competency of staff in the home.

Large complex homes with many employees will probably need more documentation than a very small home. The home can decide whether the documentation is to be in hard copy throughout, or on a computer network or intranet.

The home will have other documentation: documentation that it has decided is necessary for the efficient running of its business as well as any other documentation that is necessary because of regulations and standards that are applicable to homes.

ISO 9001 focuses on processes. A home must clearly identify its first-level processes and any interactions with other processes, be they other first-level or lower-level processes, to ensure that they collectively result in quality resident care that achieves planned results and thereby satisfies the needs and expectations of residents. Management (see Chapter 5) must ensure that adequate resources are provided and that relevant information and documentation are always available at appropriate stages during any of the processes. Above all, management has to ensure that all first-level processes and any interacting processes achieve the planned results in the most efficient manner.

Many homes are likely to have some processes in place. Most were probably introduced informally and have been amended from time to time in the light of experience, new knowledge, and new technology. Similarly, the satisfactory operation and control of such processes will have been brought to fruition in the light of such experience. Test criteria to be used at specific stages in a process may already be in place. Decisions may have been taken on appropriate monitoring and measurements that have to be made continuously or continually at different stages in a process. Any data that are collected during such processes may already be collated and analysed. Any observations, monitoring and measurements might result in corrective actions being taken to put right what is going wrong or has gone wrong. Preventive actions might also have been taken from time to time to prevent possible untoward events from happening in the future. The standard ensures that arrangements that may be informal are formally introduced and controlled systematically.

Formalization of processes and controls is not just a bureaucratic requirement. It enables top management and other staff to understand better how a home is functioning, which in turn, will provide opportunities to promote continual improvement in the effectiveness of a new quality management system of the home. This is a prime requirement of the standard.

Sometimes a home uses resources from outside to carry out tasks on its behalf. The standard refers to such action as 'outsourcing'. In the case of a residential home this would include professionals such as specialist nurses, general practitioners and dental surgeons.

A home might consider outsourcing non-professional activities when:

•   it is not a major process or core process in the home;

•   a home does not have the specialized knowledge and skills that are necessary to carry out certain processes. Whilst these could sometimes be acquired in-house it might be prohibitively expensive to do so.

Cleaning and security are early examples of outsourcing. Such services were the forerunners of today's wide-ranging outsourcing services sector, in which services are devolved to trusted external people or external organizations.

If a home outsources any services that can affect the quality of care of residents, directly or indirectly, then the home must maintain close control over such outsourcing. The means by which outsourcing is tightly controlled must be evident from the quality management system documentation of the home. In the case of professional services, the need for control extends only to being certain that access to such professionals is possible when a need arises.

Documentation requirements (ISO 9001, clause 4.2)

General (ISO 9001, clause 4.2.1)

The documentation associated with the quality management system can be conveniently divided into three main categories: the framework documentation, working documents and records (see Figure 4.1). The records are derived from both the framework documentation and from working documents. The framework documentation is the core documentation on which the quality management system is based. Working documents control all the day-to-day activities in a home that would perhaps be taking place, maybe in a different way, if a quality management system was not established. A home can only claim that a quality management system has been established when the framework documentation and the working documents exist and all employees are working in accordance with the planned arrangements as a result of the implementation of the quality management system.

The framework documentation must include a quality manual (see clause 4.2.2 and Figure 4.1). A quality policy statement is required (see Chapter 5, Figure 4.1 and the example quality policy statement on page 35). Quality objectives must be included in the framework documentation (see Chapter 5, Figure 4.1 and the example quality objectives on page 36). All of these must be controlled documents.

Six mandatory documented procedures (see Appendix 1 for details and examples) are required by the standard:

- control of documents;
- control of quality records;
- internal audit;
- control of nonconforming product;
- corrective action;
- preventive action.

The home can decide what other additional documentation is necessary to control the key aspects of the quality management system. It also has complete freedom, within the limitations imposed by any regulations and standards, to decide what documentation is required to control the planned care of residents so that they maintain and possibly achieve a better quality of life while residing in the home.

Records are also required to be kept as specified in clause 4.2.4.

The framework documentation

The framework documentation is the core documentation required to establish and maintain the quality management system. The quality management system framework documentation must include the items listed below, with suggested codes for identification and classification purposes. In addition, all documents (with the exception of the quality manual) can be numbered from, for example, 101 upwards, so that new quality management system (QMS) documents can be readily identified and distinguished from pre-QMS documents. This does not of course mean that documents with numbers below 100 are no longer relevant. These existing documents should continue to be used until the new quality management system has been established. Consideration can then be given to withdrawing any documents that have been superseded by the new quality management system documents, or if changes have to be made to existing documents, they can perhaps be re-coded and numbered in accordance with the new quality management system.

The quality management system documentation will include:

- a quality management system manual;
- quality management system process diagrams;
- the six mandatory quality management system procedures;
- quality management system policies;
- quality management system forms;
- quality management system external documents;
- quality management system external forms.

Working documents

There is another important aspect to any quality management system, namely, working documents (see Figure 4.1). These are documents that a home considers are necessary for planning, operation and control of all its processes in order to provide quality of care for all residents. First and foremost are the residents' care notes. In addition, working documents might include procedures, policies, work instructions, forms, external documents and external forms. Homes will not necessarily have all the categories of documentation listed above. For instance, some organizations may decide that few, if any, work instructions are necessary. On the other hand, management may decide that some other additional form of documentation is required to achieve the planned results or perhaps to prevent, or to minimize, the likelihood of an untoward event happening to a resident.

All homes are likely to have some external documents (other than ISO 9001 itself) issued by outside sources such as government departments and professional bodies. External documents such as regulations and standards are particularly important since they will have some bearing on the quality of care provided by the home.

Working documents will also include any external forms imposed on the home for completion for, for example, the Department of Health.

Quality manual (ISO 9001, clause 4.2.2)

A home must establish and maintain a quality management system manual. The quality manual must address the five requirement clauses of ISO 9001. These are:

Clause 4 – Quality management system;

Clause 5 – Management responsibility;

Clause 6 – Resource management;

Clause 7 – Product realization;

Clause 8 – Measurement, analysis and improvement.

Management can decide on the format of the quality manual.

A quality policy statement is required. This need not be included in the manual. It is usually signed and dated by the chief executive. An example quality quality policy statement is given on page 35. The standard requires it to be a controlled document.

Management has to ensure that quality objectives are set at relevant functions and levels within the home. These quality objectives must be measurable and can also be formally issued as a policy document (see page 35). Again, this ensures that proper control and updating are facilitated. There must be a framework in place to ensure that quality objectives are systematically reviewed. Such reviews provide opportunities for management to demonstrate its commitment to continual improvement in the effectiveness of its quality management system.

An organization chart is required. It frequently changes and can best be controlled as a policy document (see Figure 5.1).

Scope and permissible exclusions

The quality manual must include the scope of the quality management system. All the caring processes will be reflected in the scope of the quality management system documentation and, subsequently, in the scope of the ISO 9001 certificate.

The standard is intended to be generic and applicable to all kinds of organization, regardless of type and size, irrespective of the product being manufactured or the service being provided. However, it is accepted that all the requirements of ISO 9001 might not be applicable to all organizations. Clause 1.2 of ISO 9001, under Scope, states that exclusion can be considered where the requirements of the standard cannot be applied, 'due to the nature of an organization and its product'. Such exclusions are, however, limited to clause 7 and on the provision that they do not affect the organization's ability, or responsibility, to provide a service that fulfils customer and applicable regulatory requirements. If requirements are excluded that are not permissible, or if exclusion of requirements is not adequately justified, then conformity to ISO 9001 cannot be claimed and an external auditor would not be able to recommend, other things being equal, to an accredited certification body that a certificate be awarded. The exclusions must also be made clear in any other publicly available documents, such as certification documents or marketing material to avoid misleading third parties such as potential residents and families of potential residents and stakeholders.

Justifiable exclusions in a residential care home

The design and development clause (ISO 9001, clause 7.3) simply cannot be addressed for a home. See the commentary to clause 7.3 in Chapter 7.

Clause 7.5.2 of ISO 9001 (Validation of processes for production and service provision) can probably be excluded because the resulting output following application of an individual's care plan can always be validated. However, if a home has a sterilizer, depending on the type of sterilizer and its use, it is possible that this clause cannot be excluded.

Procedures

A procedure is merely the prescribed way in which an activity is carried out. Procedures can be in any form and format. Six procedures are mandatory, but management can decide for itself what other procedures are required in order to control other processes satisfactorily.

Procedures can be included in the quality manual, but it is common practice to keep procedures separate. However, appropriate cross-references must be made to procedures in the text of the manual. It is also common practice to list all the procedures in an appendix to the manual.

Interaction between processes

The quality manual will contain many processes and from these it is possible, with the supporting documentation, to understand the interaction of all processes in the quality management system. As already explained, some process diagrams have attached notes; others have links to lower-level processes.

Control of documents (ISO 9001, clause 4.2.3)

All of the documents associated with the quality management system are controlled. The proper control of documents is essential to ensure that only the approved latest documents, forms, etc. are in use, even though changes to the documentation will inevitably be necessary from time to time. The quality manager is usually made responsible for control of all the documents that are part of the organization's quality management system.

The mandatory procedure PC 101 explains how this is done (see Appendix 1).

Control of records (ISO 9001, clause 4.2.4)

Records are different from the other two groups of documentation. Records arise from the many activities that occur in a home. They provide objective evidence on what has happened. ISO 9001 requires as a minimum certain records (defined in the standard) to be kept and maintained for specified periods of time. They are referred to as records in this book. A home will have to add other records to the list such as records on residents, many of which have to be kept and maintained by statutory or regulatory requirements.

The mandatory procedure PC 102 explains how records are controlled (see Appendix 1).

The home must decide on the minimum retention times for the different kinds of record. In certain cases the times are specified by external organizations.

There must be explicit arrangements for the disposal of records after the minimum retention times have been reached.

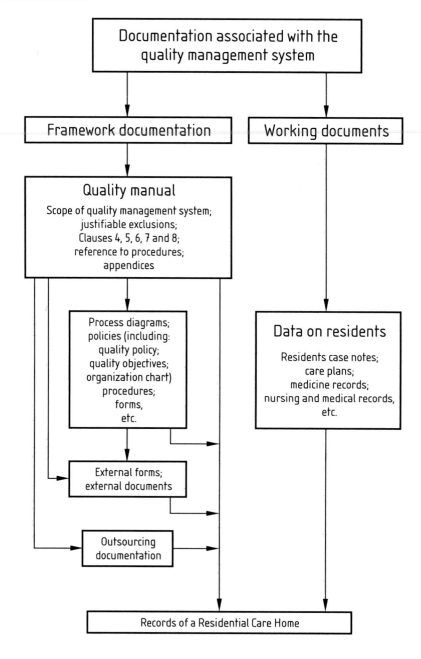

Figure 4.1 – Quality management system documentation

Chapter 5:
Management responsibility (Clause 5)

Management commitment (ISO 9001, clause 5.1)

This clause relates to regulations 7–10 [3] and standards 31–38 [4].

Every requirement in clause 5 begins, 'Top Management shall…'. In the case of residential homes this means the registered person approved by the National Care Standards Commission, who is ultimately responsible for directing and controlling a home.

ISO 9001 places explicit responsibilities on top management. This should mean that the registered person will be actively involved in the quality management system of the home and, as a result, staff members at lower levels are much more likely to take a greater interest in the quality management system of the home.

An external auditor will require objective evidence of the commitment of the registered person to the development, implementation and continuing improvement in the effectiveness of the quality management system based on ISO 9001. Top management is required to:

- establish a quality policy (see clause 5.3);

- ensure that quality objectives are set, measured and reviewed from time to time (see clause 5.4);

- conduct management reviews (see clause 5.6);

- ensure the availability of adequate resources (see clause 6.1); and

- ensure that all employees are made aware of the importance of striving at all times to improve the quality of the lives of all residents, while at the same time satisfying any statutory and regulatory requirements in connection with the quality of care of residents within a home.

It is axiomatic that the registered person for a home will be aware of statutory and regulatory requirements. If a registered person is seeking certification to ISO 9001 to maintain and improve the quality of care of residents in the home, they must also accept full responsibility for all the activities associated with the standard.

Customer focus (ISO 9001, clause 5.2)

The registered person must make every effort to satisfy the needs and expectations of residents: they expect to experience common courtesies; they expect the home to be kept clean at all times; and they expect good food and a variable diet. The registered person has to decide: how to monitor resident satisfaction; how to collect relevant information from residents; and how to examine the information collected (see Chapter 8). Many of these changes have been taking place in homes over the last few years, irrespective of ISO 9001, but the application of the standard gives further impetus to maintaining and trying to improve the quality of care for residents.

ISO 9001 focuses on processes and even this requirement might simply mean formalizing pathways that already exist. On the other hand, pathways or processes might never have been considered before. Development and/or improvement in the processes have one main aim, namely that of maintaining and improving the quality of life for residents and thereby enhancing resident satisfaction (see clauses 7.1 and 8.2.1). However, even if the introduction or improvement in the processes has little effect on the maintenance and a possible improvement in the quality of life of a resident, they will afford opportunities for rationalization of the caring activities in a home.

Quality policy (ISO 9001, clause 5.3)

The quality policy statement must be appropriate, i.e. relevant to the purpose of the home. It should contain commitments that are realistic and attainable.

The quality policy statement must include a commitment not only to satisfying the requirements of ISO 9001, but there must also be a commitment continually to improve the effectiveness of the quality management system of the home.

The quality policy statement must state that a framework exists for reviewing all measurable quality objectives in a systematic manner.

The registered person has the responsibility for ensuring that all employees (including new employees) fully understand the quality policy statement. All managers should be encouraged to discuss the implications of the quality policy statement with the people for whom they are responsible.

The registered person must systematically review the quality policy statement for its continuing suitability. It is good practice to have the quality policy on the standard agenda of management reviews (see clause 5.6) as a reminder that it is to be reviewed at least once each year. This may be at one particular review meeting in the year and also when there are changes within the home.

The quality policy statement is part of the quality management system documentation. There is no requirement for the quality policy statement to be included in the quality manual. However, it is also good practice for the quality policy statement to be made into a stand-alone policy document and displayed at strategic points within the home. It should be written on the home's headed paper, be signed by the registered person and dated, thus signifying its importance. It provides evidence to all employees and other interested parties that the registered person is committed to the home's quality management system. The quality policy statement can be uniquely identified, i.e. PL 101, Issue 1.

Planning (ISO 9001, clause 5.4)

Quality objectives (ISO 9001, clause 5.4.1)

There is a new explicit emphasis on quality objectives in ISO 9001. Quality objectives must be established at relevant functions and levels within the home. Quality objectives must be measurable and consistent with the quality policy statement. There must also be a framework for reviewing quality objectives systematically as stated in the home's quality policy statement (see clause 5.6). Such reviews provide opportunities for the registered person to demonstrate their commitment to continual improvement in the effectiveness of the quality management system.

It is good practice for the quality objectives statement to be made into a stand-alone document and displayed at strategic points within the home. As with the quality policy, the quality objectives can be uniquely identified, i.e. PL 102, Issue 1.

There are two opportunities to set quality objectives. The first is at the planning stages across the whole spectrum of a home's activities, and at different levels, including any quality objectives that specifically address maintaining and improving the quality of life of the residents. The second occasion is after implementation of the quality management system, or, if this has already been implemented, after the introduction of any new processes. Feedback from these activities might identify the need for changes to be made to quality objectives or the introduction of additional quality objectives.

It is such feedback that provides excellent opportunities for continually improving the effectiveness of the quality management system. A failure to show continual improvement in the effectiveness of the quality management system, as determined by the measurements made in connection with the quality objectives set, would indicate the need for further investigations, and perhaps for additional, or amended, quality objectives.

An external auditor from an accredited certification body would be able to raise only an observation (not a nonconformity) against a failure to achieve a quality objective, for there may be very good reasons why a home has failed to meet certain quality objectives. At the same audit, an external auditor might be completely satisfied by other objective evidence that shows that the home is nevertheless continually striving to improve the effectiveness of its quality management system.

Homes will choose different activities to focus on when setting objectives depending on what problems they face and what they consider to be the most urgent problems that need to be addressed in order to maintain and/or improve the quality of care of residents.

Quality management system planning (ISO 9001, clause 5.4.2)

When planning the quality management system, the registered person must ensure that the general requirements of the system are addressed (see clause 4.1) as well as any quality objectives such as those referred to in the previous section (5.4.1).

The registered manager must also ensure that the integrity of the quality management system is maintained when changes to the system are planned and implemented.

Responsibility, authority and communication (ISO 9001, clause 5.5)

Responsibility and authority (ISO 9001, clause 5.5.1)

The registered manager must ensure that responsibilities and authorities of all staff are defined and communicated within the home. This requirement emphasizes the obvious, namely, the need to inform staff of their responsibilities and to explain who reports to whom.

One simple and effective method of doing this is for a home organization chart to be issued (see Figure 5.1). It is given an issue number that can be increased by one each time a change takes place. There is no need for names of all staff to be included in the organization chart, but the responsibilities and authorities of senior staff must be made known throughout the home. The home's organization chart can be uniquely identified, for example, as PL 103, Issue 1.

Management representative (ISO 9001, clause 5.5.2)

The registered manager must appoint a management representative from amongst the staff. Other titles may be used for management representative, such as quality manager, quality director or quality coordinator.

The management representative has a number of defined responsibilities. First, they have to ensure that the QMS processes are established, implemented and maintained. The management representative has to report to the registered person on the performance of the quality management system and on any changes that should be made in order, for instance, to increase the operational efficiency of the home. They have to ensure the promotion of awareness of resident requirements throughout the home.

A management representative might have other related responsibilities, such as liaison with external parties on the quality management system.

In practice, a management representative plays a key role in a home's quality management system. Typical responsibilities include, among others:

(a) establishing, implementing and maintaining the quality management system;

(b) reporting to top management on the performance of the QMS and the need for changes for whatever reasons;

(c) promoting the awareness of resident requirements throughout the home;

  - The prime requirement can be expressed as the maintenance of and possible improvement in the quality of life of residents.

  - Secondary requirements include: privacy; common courtesies at all times; cleanliness at all times and in all places; and good food.

All staff members have their parts to play in achieving these requirements.

(d) Arranging, in consultation with other people, the internal audit programme; arranging internal quality audits; arranging consequential corrective and preventive actions;

(e) dealing with nonconformities: corrective and preventive actions;

(f) dealing with resident and stakeholder complaints: corrective and preventive actions;

(g) approving suppliers and subcontractors;

(h) establishing and maintaining lists of suppliers and subcontractors;

(i) controlling any calibrations of inspection, measuring and test equipment;

(j) collecting and analysing data for presentation to the management review meetings;

(k) arranging management review meetings;

(l) preparing, maintaining and archiving records and data;

(m) liaising with certification bodies and other people on all matters relating to the quality management system.

Internal communication (ISO 9001, clause 5.5.3)

The registered person must ensure that appropriate communication processes are established within the home and that the lines of communication between different people at different levels in the home and between people with different responsibilities are established and clearly understood within the home.

The registered person can choose whatever methods are considered to be most effective in establishing first-class communications with their staff. These might include:

• a meeting on the home's vision for the future;

• a meeting focusing on immediate prospects for the future;

• general meetings held on a regular basis with all staff;

• departmental meetings;

• meetings that focus on feedback from staff;

• meetings on the suggestion scheme awards;

• merit recognition meetings;

• use of notice boards for imparting important information;

• in-house journals or magazines.

Regular meetings might be held exclusively in connection with ISO 9001 at which any aspect of the quality management system can be discussed.

Specifically, feedback directly to the registered person regarding the effectiveness of the quality management system should be encouraged. This might be achieved through such regular meetings, through individual representations, or through written submissions. The registered person should stress to all employees the importance of such feedback.

Management review (ISO 9001, clause 5.6)

General (ISO 9001, clause 5.6.1)

The registered person must review the home's quality management system, at planned intervals, to ensure its continuing suitability, adequacy and effectiveness. The review must include assessing opportunities for improvement and the need for changes to the system, including changes to the quality policy and quality objectives.

There is no requirement regarding the frequency of management reviews. The home can decide on the planned interval between such meetings. However, it is evident that meetings that are held only annually cannot be of any real value to a home. This certainly would not allow the registered person to be in control of its quality management system. As a result, they would be depriving themselves of a valuable management tool.

Extraordinary management review meetings may, of course, be called at any time by the registered person, but the standard agenda need not be used on such occasions.

The management representative will play a leading role in the preparations for the meetings and in the ensuing discussions.

Management review meetings must be recorded. The customary method is by means of minutes that include the findings of the reviews, the actions to be taken and the names of persons responsible for carrying through such actions by specified dates. Records of all management reviews become part of records (see clause 4.2.4 and Figure 4.1).

The standard identifies items for inclusion in the agenda of management review meetings (see clause 5.6.2) and, through the output clause (see clause 5.6.3), requires decisions and corresponding actions to be identified. Well organized homes already do this through a comprehensive agenda and proper minutes of meetings in which decisions are recorded with accompanying actions and dates for completion.

Review input (ISO 9001, clause 5.6.2)

This clause lists items that must be included in any management reviews:

(a) follow-up actions from previous management reviews;

(b) results of audits;

(c) improvements in resident pathways and achievements in quality of life of residents;

(d) status of preventive and corrective actions;

(e) resident feedback (i.e. resident complaints and resident satisfaction surveys);

(f) recommendations for improvement;

(g) changes that could affect the quality management system.

Review output (ISO 9001, clause 5.6.3)

The outputs from the management review must include decisions and actions related to:

(a) improvement in the effectiveness of the quality management system and its processes;

(b) any changes likely to improve the quality of life of residents;

(c) resource needs.

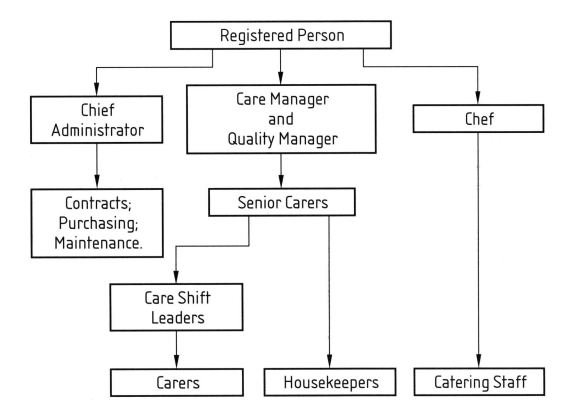

Figure 5.1 – Organizational chart

A typical agenda for a management review meeting

1. Apologies for absence

2. Approval of the minutes of the previous management review meeting

3. Matters arising from the previous minutes, not covered by the agenda below

4. Internal audits: schedule; results of audits; corrective and preventive actions

5. External audits/surveillances by certification body

6. Performance of processes

7. Nonconformities: corrective and preventive actions

8. Resident feedback:

   - resident complaints;

   - corrective actions;

   - preventive actions;

   - monitoring of residents' satisfaction

9. Review of quality objectives

10. Purchasing: lists of suppliers and subcontractors

11. Human resources:

    - competence requirements

    - training needs

    - evaluation of training

    - skills testing

12. Analysis of data

13. Changes that could affect the quality management system

14. Review of quality policy on a systematic basis (and as and when deemed necessary)

15. Continual improvements in the effectiveness of the quality management system

16. Suggestions for improvements in the effectiveness of the processes: major processes with attached notes and any lower-level processes

17. Future resource needs

18. Any other business

19. Date of next meeting

NOTE Time might not permit all the items on the agenda to be addressed at one meeting. Those not addressed can be given some preference at the subsequent meeting.

Quality policy

The Residential Care Home has 59 single en-suite rooms in a modern building situated in Anytown in the heart of Berkshire. It provides first-class accommodation and care for elderly people, men and women, in a caring and friendly environment.

The home is well staffed with experienced carers with an unusually high staff/resident ratio. The home prides itself in first-class management.

All staff at the home are committed to excellence based on the international quality management systems standard, ISO 9001. All staff are committed to continual improvement in the effectiveness of its quality management system.

Measurable quality objectives are in place. They are reviewed on a regular basis in a systematic manner at management review meetings.

The home strives at all times to satisfy the needs of residents. Resident satisfaction is monitored so that improvements can be made whenever any shortcomings are identified.

All staff, including new employees, are made aware of the home's quality management system and are expected to implement, maintain and adhere to its requirements. Everyone is encouraged to suggest ways in which the quality management system can be improved.

The management of the home will review this quality policy statement at least annually or earlier when considered to be appropriate.

Date:_____ Signed:_____

The Registered Person, Residential Care Home

Quality objectives

(Each care home must decide for itself what are the most important objectives that should be set for, for example, the ensuing year. Those given below are merely suggestions.)

Care home's overall objectives

To reduce the number of residents' complaints by 20% during 2005.

To establish by January 2006 an independent review stage for complainants who remain dissatisfied by the response they have received from the attempts to resolve matters locally.

Objectives for carers

All carers will attend at least three training courses of their own choosing each year.

(This is in addition to the compulsory courses.)

Date: .... Signed: ....

The Registered Person, Residential Care Home

Chapter 6:
Resource management (Clause 6)

Provision of resources (ISO 9001, clause 6.1)

Resources can be classified as: human resources, physical resources (e.g. equipment), the infrastructure and the work environment. All of these resources contribute towards helping a home to achieve its overall goals and specific objectives.

The registered person must determine and provide resources needed to implement and maintain the quality management system, with a focus on continual improvement in the effectiveness of the system to enhance resident satisfaction.

The registered person must also determine and provide the resources needed to enhance resident satisfaction by helping carers to maintain and, whenever possible, improve the quality of care for residents. Management must also enable other staff to provide all the other services that are indirectly associated with quality resident care.

Human resources (ISO 9001, clause 6.2)

This clause relates to regulations 18 and 19 [3], schedule 2, and standards 27–30 [4].

General (ISO 9001, clause 6.2.1)

All employees whose duties and responsibilities might have a bearing on the quality of resident care in homes must be competent in the tasks that they have to carry out, as determined by their relevant education, training, skills and experience.

Competence, awareness and training (ISO 9001, clause 6.2.2)

The registered person must determine the necessary competences required for all personnel performing activities that have a bearing on the quality of life of residents in the care home.

Most carers have few if any qualifications and most residential care homes have to provide training for suitably selected carers in particular, as well as for other staff such as cleaners. After such training, the previously defined competences of those who have undergone training can be checked. In cases in which competence has not reached the accepted standard, some kind of further training or other actions may be necessary in order to be certain that staff do have the previously defined competences. A failure to attain the requirement competences, for whatever reason, means that the person must be re-deployed on less demanding tasks, or their employment must be terminated.

Only when a carer has been proved to be competent in the specified skills for carers can they be allowed to work alone, caring for a resident.

The training provided must be evaluated, since the failure to become competent in a particular activity might be the result of poor delivery of a course or possibly because very important points might have been omitted from the course.

Potential trainees for additional training can be identified through an appraisal scheme. One such method is to ask employees to undertake a self-appraisal each year using a prescribed form. Afterwards, employees are subjected to an appraisal, which is conducted in a prescribed manner by a more senior member of staff. Both completed forms are held as confidential quality records. When management is looking for further staff to train in order to acquire additional specific competences such records on appraisals are invaluable.

Appropriate records are maintained of education, qualifications, training, experience, and competency skills for all staff, as well as the evaluation records of any training courses undertaken (see clause 4.2.4).

All employees must be made aware of the relevance and importance of the work that they are doing in contributing towards achieving the quality objectives of the home (see clause 5.4.1) within the framework of ISO 9001.

Infrastructure (ISO 9001, clause 6.3)

This clause relates to regulation 23 [3] and standards 19–26 [4].

Management determines, provides and maintains the infrastructure needed to ensure that the quality of care of residents is maintained and, whenever possible, improved.

The infrastructure includes:

(a) safe, clean, odourless, well maintained, buildings;

(b) safe and adequate heating, lighting and ventilation throughout;

(c) safe and controlled water temperatures at all times;

(d) residents' own rooms: safe and comfortable rooms including, if wanted, space for some of their own furniture;

(e) adequate number of suitable lavatories and washing facilities;

(f) safe and comfortable communal indoor and outdoor facilities;

(g) appropriate devices and equipment, e.g. lifts, to enhance independence of others;

(h) adequate supporting services (as opposed to carers) such as cleaners.

The home's guide or other documentation should address these points.

Work environment (ISO 9001, clause 6.4)

The home also has to ensure that all employees work in a generally acceptable environment that is conducive to encouraging employees to give of their best in terms of residential care. Relevant factors include:

(a) safety of individuals (staff and residents);

(b) ergonomics of working;

(c) appropriate lighting levels;

(d) appropriate temperature and humidity levels;

(e) acceptable noise levels;

(g) acceptable levels of cleanliness and hygiene;

(h) minimum pollution levels;

(i) provision of appropriate protective equipment.

Many of these factors are the subject of legislation, regulation or codes of practice.

The management of the home must ensure that appropriate controls are in place to maintain the planned work environments.

Chapter 7:
Product realization (Clause 7)

Planning of product realization (ISO 9001, clause 7.1)

'Product realization' is the term used to encompass all of the activities between establishing the needs of a potential resident (process diagram PD 101) and the preparation of an individual care plan (process diagrams PD 102 and PD 103). It is the individual care plans that are key to maintaining and, whenever possible, improving the quality of life of a prospective resident, although the general provisions in a home also make an important contribution to the quality of life of a resident.

Quality objectives need to be set for the registered person and other staff.

All the process diagrams are an integral part of the quality management system of the home. These include any notes attached to a process diagram and any lower-level processes. The human and physical resources specific to the needs and care of residents must be identified. Any monitoring, inspection and test activities required must be identified. It is unlikely that any monitoring or measuring devices will need to be calibrated in a typical home, apart from, say, one thermometer to be used as a secondary standard. Verification of the continuing service provided will be achieved through informal daily monitoring by management and formal planned audits under ISO 9001. Validation of the output of the services provided in terms of the maintenance and, wherever possible, improvements in the quality of life for residents will be sought through questionnaires and feedback from residents and their relatives.

If a home decides to outsource any process that can have a bearing on the maintenance of and improvements in the quality of life for residents, the home must ensure control over such processes. An example of outsourcing might be an independent cleaning contractor. Professionals need not be controlled, but the availability of such people must be guaranteed.

Decisions are required on the records that will be kept. Such records (see clause 4.2.4), will provide objective evidence that the home's processes are being followed as planned. Other records will give confidence that the individual care plans are being followed as planned, apart from changes deemed necessary and initiated by the care manager who has overall responsibility for resident care (Regulation 17 and Schedules 3 and 4 [3]).

If planned changes to the quality management system are implemented, the integrity of the system must be maintained at all times [see clause 5.4.2 (b)].

Any individual care plans and training plans should be structured so that everyone is made aware of the need to improve continually the effectiveness of the quality management system. All employees of the home should be told that suggestions for such improvements will always be welcomed by the registered person.

Customer-related processes (ISO 9001, clause 7.2)

This clause relates to regulation 4 and schedule 1; regulations 5.1 and standard 1.2; regulations 6 and 22 and standards 1 to 5 [3 and 4].

Determination of requirements related to the product (ISO 9001, clause 7.2.1)

The needs of a potential resident can be summed up by the need to maintain and, whenever possible, improve their quality of life. The importance of establishing the needs of an elderly person before they take up long-term residence in a home is, therefore, of paramount importance. If a person is allowed to enter a home before it has been established beyond all reasonable doubt that the needs can be met, there is a chance that the individual might be very dissatisfied with the home, and the quality of life of the new resident might deteriorate and become unacceptable.

Initially, the onus is on the registered person to help a prospective resident following the first enquiries about a home. All registered residential care homes must have a statement of purpose. The statement of purpose sent to a prospective resident must include specific information. This is listed in note 2 attached to the process diagram PD 101 (Regulation 4 (1) and Schedule 1). A prospective resident must also be sent a resident's guide to the home. Again, the detailed requirements are listed in note 2 (Regulation 5 (1) and Standard 1.2).

The statement of purpose and the resident's guide are very important documents in that they must provide reliable information that a prospective resident will want to know when considering which home to choose.

The registered manager must keep these documents under review and if changes are made to either of them the National Care Standards Commission must be advised within 28 days of any such changes (Regulation 6).

If any general enquiry subsequently leads to a specific enquiry about possible long-term residence, the care manager or a senior carer will establish the precise needs of the prospective resident. These will be documented in a proposed individual care plan (see clause 7.5.2). If it becomes evident that certain needs of a potential resident could not be met, they are advised accordingly.

Any enquires about short-term care and emergency admissions will be dealt with in the same way.

Review of requirements related to the product (ISO 9001, clause 7.2.2)

The registered person or the care manager must formally review both the needs and the prepared care plan of a potential resident before a contract is signed. The outcome of all such review processes must be that the needs of residents are fully documented and understood and it is agreed that those needs can be met. Only after this has been done can a prospective resident be formally advised that the needs can be met through an individual care plan. If the enquirer wishes to pursue the matter further, a contract can be prepared (Standard 2).

If needs change during the contract stage, a further review is necessary to re-confirm that the revised needs can be met by modification of the resident's care plan.

The review process and any subsequent changes must be fully documented (see clause 4.2.4).

Customer communication (ISO 9001, clause 7.2.3)

The standard requires management to determine and implement effective channels of communication between the home and its residents (or their nominees) on all matters.

Resident feedback can be either verbal, or written. It can be reactive or proactive. Resident complaints that are reactive to some occurrence or non-occurrence must be dealt with in a systematic manner (see clauses 8.5.2). An example of a proactive case is the monitoring of resident satisfaction (see clause 8.2.1). Whatever the nature of the feedback from residents, arrangements must be in place for dealing with it in a systematic manner (see mandatory procedures, PC 104, PC 105 and PC 106).

Design and development (ISO 9001, clause 7.3)

The design and development clause 7.3 can be justifiably excluded from the quality management system when ISO 9001 is applied to residential care homes. This decision is justified by an examination of the different clauses.

Clause 7.3 contains the following clauses:

7.3.1   Design and development planning

7.3.2   Design and development inputs

7.3.3   Design and development outputs

7.3.4   Design and development review

7.3.5   Design and development verification

When addressing the question of possible justifiable exclusion, it is important to appreciate that up to and including clause 7.3.5, no service would have been provided.

Clause 7.3.6 Design and development validation

This clause certainly has to be discussed during the first five stages of any design and development proposal.

Clause 7.3.7 Control of design and development changes

It is inevitable that during the design and development stages some changes might be requested by any party associated with a design project. It is very important that any such requests for changes at any stage of a project should be fully documented and, if any changes are agreed, all interested parties sign to that effect.

Application of ISO 9001, clauses 7.3.1 to 7.3.7, in the case of care homes

Clause 7.3.2 can be addressed in that the needs of residents are carefully determined and specified in a care plan, as explained in the commentary to clause 7.2.1.

The purpose of clause 7.3.3 is to ensure that the outcomes are certain before any caring begins. Unfortunately, in the case of care homes, the outcomes cannot be certain until after some caring has taken place, because one is dealing with people and the expected maintenance of the quality of life, a subjective matter (particularly in relation to the requirement to, whenever possible, improve the quality of life of residents). Thus, it is impossible to apply clause 7.3.3 to the residents of care homes. Of course, the care manager in consultation with the staff of the home, the resident, and possibly the relatives will make changes to the care plan in the hope that the resident's quality of life will be maintained as expected, and, perhaps, that it will be improved. This requires intelligent on-going informed guesswork, in the hope that success will eventually be achieved. If the key clause 7.3.3 cannot be addressed then the whole of the design and development clause 7.3 becomes irrelevant.

Nevertheless, consider the subsequent clauses. The review of needs for a potential resident that the care manager undertakes, referred to in relation to clause 7.2.2, is merely a check to ensure that the home can meet the detailed day-to-day needs of a resident, as might eventually be specified in a contract between the home and a potential resident. As explained earlier, it cannot guarantee that the output will definitely be satisfactory before the resident enters the home and care for the new resident commences. However, the purpose of clause 7.3.4 is to ensure that before a service begins, an organization must be certain that the designed output will indeed meet the designed input. As explained in the previous paragraph this cannot be certain. Thus, clause 7.3.4 cannot be addressed in the case of a residential care home.

Similarly, clause 7.3.5, Design and development verification, cannot be addressed before the elderly person becomes a resident, simply because, as explained, the home is dealing with people, and outcomes in terms of maintenance of quality of life is a subjective matter.

Validation (clause 7.3.6) is the means by which both parties to a contract are to confirm that the actual output (the manufactured product or the service delivered) does in fact satisfy the finally agreed and documented requirements. Discussions on validation can take place before any action commences or during the action stages. In the case of a resident in a home, the output, as explained earlier, is subjective and not definitive so this clause cannot be addressed satisfactorily.

The purpose of clause 7.3.7 is to ensure that changes can be made to the design, in this case, of a service, at any stage, and can be proposed by either party to an earlier agreement, provided that any agreed changes are fully documented and signed by both parties. However, since as explained earlier, the output clause cannot be addressed satisfactorily, this clause is irrelevant.

Purchasing (ISO 9001, clause 7.4)

Purchasing process (ISO 9001, clause 7.4.1)

Suppliers and subcontractors that provide products and/or services that will not have any bearing on the maintenance of, or improvement in, the quality of life of residents in the home need not be subjected to the same scrutiny as outlined in this chapter. On the other hand, food is an important purchase. There may be others, but it is for the home to decide what purchases and services need to be carefully controlled in accordance with the requirements of ISO 9001. These requirements are explained below.

A home must ensure that a purchased product or service conforms to specified purchase requirements. A home must evaluate potential suppliers and subcontractors on this basis. There are many ways in which this can be done, such as:

- questionnaires;

- visits to the home by a potential supplier or subcontractor;

- conducting an audit on those activities of the supplier or subcontractor that are of particular interest;

- placement of a trial order;

- seeking the opinions of others.

Homes can choose the ways in which suppliers and subcontractors are evaluated, but the criteria for evaluation, selection and any necessary re-evaluations must be defined.

The results of evaluations and selections and any subsequent follow-up actions must be recorded and held as records (see clause 4.2.4).

In practical terms, after evaluation and selection, many homes establish an approved list of suppliers and subcontractors. Some also have a temporary list. The temporary list includes suppliers and subcontractors that are being used and will probably be transferred to the approved list in due course. Transfer to the approved list can take place after a satisfactory track record has been established, or after a second party audit has been conducted, or by whatever other means are considered appropriate.

Some homes also have a non-approved list, which includes suppliers and subcontractors that have not met the required standards of the home and that must not be used by any employees.

The performance of chosen suppliers should be reviewed on a regular basis and the lists should be updated as necessary. Evidence of updating should be available.

Purchasing information (ISO 9001, clause 7.4.2)

Purchase orders and associated documents must always contain all the information that a supplier or a subcontractor will need in order to satisfy the home's requirements. Any associated documentation, referred to in the purchase order, will stress any conditional requirements of placing the order.

Verbal orders always need to be followed by documented purchase orders and associated documentation so that both parties are fully aware of what has been ordered and under what conditions.

Most homes clearly describe on their purchase orders (and any associated documents) what is required and have designated levels of authority to review and approve such orders. This is not a very onerous requirement. In simple cases, it is implicit that the person signing the order has, as a minimum, looked at the order and given an approval of adequacy, as would be the case for standard off-the-shelf items, which are unlikely to pose problems. However, in the case of complex orders for a manufactured product, or a sophisticated service, the home might have to impose some sort of checklist, each section of which would have to be signed off by named signatories, before a final signature is added by a purchasing manager, or in the case of very big orders by the registered person for the home. Each home must decide what is appropriate for its own circumstances within the remit of the standard.

Verification of purchased product (ISO 9001, clause 7.4.3)

The nature and extent of the controls applied to a selected supplier or subcontractor will depend on the effect the purchased product, or service provided, has on the maintenance and possible improvement of the quality of life of residents. Some purchased products or services that are regarded by the home as being crucial to the success of its caring processes are likely to be subjected to strict controls. Others that are much less important will be subject to less stringent controls.

The activities necessary for verification of purchased product must be identified and implemented. In many cases, if the supplier or subcontractor has an established track record with the home, the verification of a product on receipt, or provision of a service, at the home will be minimal. On the other hand, with a new supplier, the home might well impose strict verification processes; these will be identified in advance and implemented on receipt of goods or when the service is being provided.

Production and service provision (ISO 9001, clause 7.5)

Control of production and service provision (ISO 9001, clause 7.5.1)

All the activities and services associated with a residential care home need to be planned and thereafter suitably controlled to ensure that planned provisions are adhered to in all respects. How this control is achieved is for the home to decide, within any statutory and regulatory requirements.

Choosing a residential home

This information here relates to regulation 4 and schedule 1; regulations 5.1 and standard 1.2; regulations 6 and 22 and standards 1–5 [3 and 4].

Clause 7.2 and PD 101 outline the steps that are to be taken to provide prospective residents with information to help them to choose a suitable residential care home.

Care plan

The information here relates to regulation 15 [3] and standards 3 and 7 [4].

Once the needs of a resident have been established, the registered person is responsible for ensuring that an individual care plan (see clause 7.2.1) is created for each resident.

A few important steps in the preparation of care plans are shown in process diagram 102 (first-level). PD 102 level 2 identifies the points that should be considered when preparing a care plan that will maintain and possibly improve the quality of life of a resident.

Health of residents

The information here relates to standard 8 [4].

When a resident enters a home one of the many underlying assumptions is that the health of the resident will be maintained within the limitations of human endeavours. The registered person for the home accepts this responsibility and ensures access to health care services whenever necessary. There are many possible needs, but care staff need to pay particular attention to the following.

- Personal and oral hygiene
  Whenever possible, carers encourage residents to care for themselves, unless there is evidence that a resident needs help in these respects.

- Pressure sores
  Care staff are trained to identify pressure sores, or the development of pressure sores, with appropriate intervention, which will be recorded on an updated care plan. The outcomes are also recorded in the resident's care plan. Appropriate equipment should be available for the promotion of tissue viability and for prevention, or treatment, of pressure sores.

- Incontinence
  Care staff are trained to seek professional advice, when necessary, about the promotion of continence. Aids and equipment are provided to deal with incontinence.

- Psychological state
  The psychological health of residents is monitored regularly. Preventive and restorative care is provided when deemed necessary.

- Exercise
  Opportunities are provided for residents to take appropriate exercise. Appropriate interventions are in place for residents who are at risk of falling.

- Nutrition
  Nutritional screening is undertaken on admission and subsequently on a periodic basis. Records are maintained on nutrition, including weight gain or loss. Appropriate action is taken when weight loss or gain is found.

- GP registration
  All residents are registered, preferably with a GP of their choice.

- Specialist services: hospitals and community services
  All residents have access to specialist medical, nursing, dental, pharmaceutical, chiropody and therapeutic services and care from hospitals and community health services according to need.

- Hearing and sight tests
  All residents have access to hearing and sight tests and appropriate aids according to need.

- Entitlements and guidance on NHS services
  Residents' entitlements to NHS services are upheld in accordance with guidance and legislation, including the standards in the National Service Framework, by providing information about entitlements and ensuring access to advice.

Medication

The information here relates to regulation 13 [3] and standard 9 [4].

The registered person must ensure that the home has a procedure for medication.

Care staff must be given basic training in the use and hazards associated with medicines. In particular they must know:

- how medicines are handled;

- how records on medicines and medication taken are kept;

- how to monitor residents on self-medication; and

- (in the event of a resident's condition deteriorating that might be associated with medication) how to seek medical guidance and help without delay.

All drugs in the control of the home must be handled in accordance with legislation, and guidelines. Effective controls must be in place to ensure that all drugs entering the home are properly controlled in a safe manner at all times with appropriate documentation.

Self-medication is permissible by residents following a satisfactory assessment that the resident will not be placed at unnecessary risk. Medication must be stored in lockable cupboards in the resident's own room. If self-medication is not possible, medication is administered by senior carers. Administration of medicine to residents undergoing nursing care must be carried out by a registered nurse or by a general practitioner.

Much tighter controls are necessary for controlled drugs, both as regards storage and administration. Controlled drugs can be administered only by a registered nurse or a general practitioner. The administration of a controlled drug is always witnessed by another designated person and appropriately trained member of staff. An entry is made in the controlled drugs register after administration of a controlled drug.

After the death of a resident, drugs should be retained for a period of seven days (see 'Dying and death' later in this chapter).

Social contacts and activities
The information here relates to regulation 16 [3] and standards 15, 14, 12 and 13 [4].

Meals and mealtimes
Residents should have a varied, appealing, wholesome and nutritious diet according to individually assessed and recorded requirements. All meals must be provided in a congenial setting and at various times.

Each resident must be offered three meals each day, at least one of which must be cooked, at intervals of not exceeding five hours.

Hot and cold drinks and snacks must be available at all times and offered regularly. A snack meal must be offered in the evening and the interval between this and breakfast the following morning must not exceed 12 hours.

Food, including liquefied meals, should be presented in a manner that is attractive and appealing in terms of texture, flavour and appearance, in order to maintain appetite and nutrition.

There must be a menu that is changed regularly, offering a choice of meals in a suitable format that is given to and, if necessary, read and explained to residents.

Sufficient time must be given to residents to eat their meals. If residents need help in eating their food, assistance will be given in a discreet and sensitive manner.

When advised by health care and dietetic staff, special therapeutic diets/feeds will be provided, including provision of calcium and vitamin D.

Religious and cultural dietary needs are catered for on special occasions as agreed prior to admission and laid down in the resident's care plan.

Autonomy and choice
The home is organized so that residents can exercise maximum personal autonomy and choice:

• in financial affairs;

• in contacting external agents or bodies (the home can provide advice if required to residents, their families and friends);

- by allowing residents to bring personal possessions into the home, subject to agreement prior to taking up residence;

- by allowing residents to examine their own records in the home (Data Protection Act, 1988).

Daily living in the home

The in-house daily living and activities that are made available must be flexible and varied to suit residents' expectations, preferences and capabilities. Choices should include:

- leisure and social activities and cultural interests;

- routines of daily living;

- personal and social relationships;

- religious observance.

Residents' interests will have been recorded in their individual files, and residents are given opportunities to pursue them. Residents with disabilities (dementia and other cognitive impairments, and visual and hearing impairments) will be encouraged to make the most of any appropriate and stimulating activities provided by the home.

All the planned activities in the home are well publicized.

Community activities

Residents are encouraged to have visitors from the community. They may be seen privately, with others or not at all. Management does not impose any restrictions on visitors unless requested by residents and recorded as such.

Involvement by local community groups and/or volunteers must be in accord with the wishes of residents.

Complaints

The information here relates to regulation 22 [3] and standards 16 and 17 [4].

Complaints from residents or their families are addressed in Chapter 8 (see clause 8.5 and PD 104).

Privacy and dignity

The information here relates to regulation 12 [3] and standard 10 [4].

Satisfying the needs of a resident includes giving an assurance that the resident's privacy and dignity will be respected at all times. This is such an important requirement that a number of points are highlighted:

- Personal care
  Whilst washing; whilst using the toilet or commode; whilst bathing; whilst receiving nursing care.

- Limited access
  To own room; own bathroom and toilet.

- Medical examinations and treatment
  These must be conducted in a resident's own room.

- Consultations
  Privacy during discussions with and examinations by health and social care professionals.
  Privacy when with legal and financial advisers.

- Maintenance of contacts
  Privacy with family; with relatives; with friends.

- Communication
  Residents must have easy access to telephones for private conversations.
  All mail must be given to residents unopened.

- Dress
  Residents should wear their own clothes.

- Terms of address
  These should be formal, friendly and respectful. If a resident asks to be called by a first name, or even a nickname, such a request should be granted and made known to other staff and, with the resident's permission, to other residents.

- Shared rooms
  Suitable screening must be provided to ensure that privacy is not compromised when personal care, medical examinations or treatment are being given.

Dying and death

The information here relates to regulation 37 [3] and standard 11 [4].

A residential care home for older people is expected to have documentation in place relating to residents who are dying and for those who have died.

All staff must be willing and able to talk sensitively and act appropriately when the death of a resident occurs.

All residents who are dying, and who are therefore more vulnerable than is normally the case, should receive extra special care. This means that whenever possible:

(a) immediately before death:

- their privacy and dignity is maintained;

- their wishes are addressed as far as is possible;

- they are made as comfortable as possible;

- pain relief is administered;

- they continue to live in their own rooms, surrounded by familiar objects;

- their wishes immediately prior to and after death are established and documented, whenever possible, perhaps with the help of relatives and friends;

- home staff and other residents are encouraged to give support;

- professional help in dealing with the dying and death can be made available;

- relatives and friends can stay with the dying resident for as long as they wish;

(b) immediately after death:

- time is allowed for family and friends to pay their respects;

- the body of the resident is handled in a dignified and secure manner;

- bereavement counselling can be provided.

Validation of processes for production and service provision (ISO 9001, clause 7.5.2)

It is always possible to determine retrospectively whether the care plan devised for a specific resident has resulted in the maintenance of, or possible improvement in, the quality of life of a resident. This can be achieved through observing the resident and by discussions with the resident and/or with the resident's relatives. As mentioned earlier, the maintenance of the quality of life is a subjective matter, but hopefully in most circumstances a consensus can be reached amongst those involved in the investigation. What is most important in this context is that, where there is some doubt about the current outcome, the personalized care plan can be changed in the hope of achieving better results.

This clause can be justifiably excluded from a home's quality management system since the resulting outputs following the application of the personalized care plan can always be validated by subsequent observations and discussions with the resident and/or the resident's relatives.

Identification and traceability (ISO 9001, clause 7.5.3)

Identification

Residential care homes should identify their residents by using the agreed name of the resident.

It is advisable to maintain records of any identification data that are used (see clause 4.2.4 and PC 102).

Traceability

The information here relates to standard 9 [4].

If traceability is explicitly required on any items or processes, the home must control and record the unique identification of individual items, or batches of items, as is considered appropriate. This is particularly the case for general medication and for controlled drugs.

Whilst traceability is a requirement or essential in some cases, it can also be useful in much less onerous circumstances. For example, in the case of a cleaning service, a home often considers it useful to be able to identify which cleaners did what on certain dates and, thereby, provide full traceability on the service provided.

It is advisable to maintain records on all traceability data used (see clause 4.2.4).

Customer property (ISO 9001, clause 7.5.4) (Standard 35)

The home must ensure that due care is exercised with the property of residents. This includes any money given to the home for safe-keeping.

Any confidential information provided by a resident must be respected as such.

If a resident's property is lost or damaged, then this must be reported to the resident (see clause 4.2.4)

Preservation of product (ISO 9001, clause 7.5.5)

General

As explained earlier, the product of a home is the maintenance and possible improvement in the quality of life of a resident. Every effort must be made at all times whilst a resident is in the home to ensure that the quality of life of the resident is not allowed to deteriorate in any way.

Identification

As explained in the commentary to clause 7.5.3, the onus is placed on a home following discussion with a resident/relative on how best to uniquely identify residents.

Handling

The home must at all times handle residents carefully so that residents (and staff) are not injured, whilst they are being lifted or handled in any way.

Packaging

Not applicable.

Storage

Not applicable.

Protection

A home is expected to provide protection for its residents from malicious damage, assault, etc. whilst within the confines of the home. A home is also expected to provide protection of property against damage, theft, etc.

(In the event of a resident dying, certain measures must be in place to ensure the remains of the deceased are treated in a dignified manner. Access to the mortuary must be properly controlled so that corpses are protected and accorded a secure resting place.)

Preservation

A home must ensure that all residents are adequately cared for at all times.

Delivery

Homes sometimes have to move residents within the confines of a home. Sometimes residents have to be transferred to other homes, or to other places for treatment, for example, by a dental surgeon. Care must be exercised to ensure that this is always done in a safe manner.

Control of monitoring and measuring devices (ISO 9001, clause 7.6)

It is important to differentiate between measurement and monitoring.

There is little doubt about what is meant by measurement. Measurement is associated with determination of, for example, length, area, volume, time, speed, velocity, acceleration, weight and temperature.

If measuring devices are being used to monitor a resident's condition, the monitoring might be taking place continuously. Such measuring devices immediately identify any untoward changes that are taking place so that appropriate action can be taken immediately. If the changes or trends are taking place slowly they give early warning of problems.

Monitoring, using measuring devices, is not always done continuously. It might be done continually, i.e. from time to time, as determined by a protocol or as determined by the care nurse who is responsible for the care of a particular resident. Monitoring, however, does not always involve measuring devices. For instance, ISO 9001 requires a home to monitor (not measure) resident satisfaction. This can be done without measuring devices (see clause 8.2.1).

Residents in care homes undergo few measurements by care staff. These might include weight and temperature. There is no need to have such devices calibrated. If, however, an unusual and unexpected result is obtained, the measurement should be repeated by another similar device. If there is a serious discrepancy, the suspected faulty device should either be repaired or be disposed of.

Routine maintenance is important in some cases. For instance, traditional sphygmomanometers need to undergo maintenance, because of the wear and tear that they experience in frequent use. They do not have to be calibrated since they provide only a crude measurement of blood pressure and are subject to human measuring errors.

The temperatures of refrigerators that contain food or drugs need to be controlled and maximum and minimum thermometers need to be fitted. These do not have to be calibrated, but a calibrated thermometer should be available for making systematic checks on such thermometers. Records must be maintained on the calibrated thermometer, preferably certificated by a UKAS calibration laboratory. Records must be maintained on the checks that are made on the refrigerators (see clause 4.2.4).

Chapter 8:
Measurement, analysis and improvement (Clause 8)

General (ISO 9001, clause 8.1)

Management must plan and implement monitoring, measurement, analysis and improvement processes needed:

- to ensure conformity of the quality management system with the requirements of the standard;

- to improve continually the effectiveness of the quality management system of the home; and

- to demonstrate conformity of home processes that have the objective of maintaining and, whenever possible, improving the quality of life of residents.

As explained in section 7.6, probably the only measurement that is made of residents is their weight. The temperature of food and medicine refrigerators has to be monitored to ensure that it remains within acceptable limits at all times. Hence the need for maximum and minimum thermometers to be fitted to food and medicine refrigerators.

Data on all such measurements must be recorded. In planning any monitoring and measuring activities, due consideration must always be given to deciding how the data collected are to be used.

Monitoring and measurement (ISO 9001, clause 8.2)

Customer satisfaction (ISO 9001, clause 8.2.1)

A residential care home is required to monitor (not measure) resident satisfaction in a proactive manner, to determine whether resident satisfaction has been achieved. Each home can decide for itself how it monitors resident satisfaction, although the methods used for obtaining and using the information have to be set out and explained. The monitoring must focus on resident perceptions of whether the home has met resident requirements (see clause 7.2.1).

Information on resident satisfaction can be obtained in a number of ways. Some examples follow.

1. **Direct communication with residents**

    The standard method of obtaining information from residents regarding their satisfaction is for a home to issue a form to residents and ask them to complete it and return it to the responsible person for the home. Such forms can vary enormously in their complexity, but the more complex the form the less likely it is to be completed.

    Although collection of information, or feedback from residents, might be considered to have been reasonably successful, the analysis of such data to provide a true measure of the success of the home in satisfying the needs of residents is a task that needs to be undertaken in a careful manner. Any analysis highlights the importance of asking the right questions, and often after receipt of the first batch of completed questionnaires, changes will need to be made to a questionnaire to improve the feedback from residents. Homes are advised to keep their questionnaires very simple with only a few carefully thought out questions. Large organizations can use questionnaires that have many more questions. The answers can be entered into a computer and computer analysis is clearly helpful in obtaining indicators of resident satisfaction.

    The analyses of resident satisfaction questionnaires should be considered at management reviews when weaknesses and strengths will be highlighted, and perhaps new quality objectives can be set for the ensuing period.

2. **Telephone enquiries to relatives of residents**

    Another method is to telephone, for example every three months, a given percentage of the relatives of residents and ask them to answer a set of questions.

Homes should also take note of secondary sources of indications of satisfaction of people in resident care homes:

3. **Independent investigations**

    In the UK one such source is the *Which?* reports published by the Consumers' Association and media investigations such as the BBC 'Watchdog' programmes.

4. **Press reports**

    Journalists often highlight dissatisfaction of individuals or groups of individuals. Such secondary sources of indications of satisfaction, or more likely dissatisfaction, will probably be applicable perhaps to only one home. All homes should be aware of such adverse reports so that the problems highlighted are not allowed to occur in their homes.

Relying on resident complaints to give an indication of resident satisfaction, however well organized, is unlikely to give the complete picture. A relatively small number of complaints received and recorded may be only the tip of an iceberg as far as resident dissatisfaction is concerned.

In all cases of resident dissatisfaction there may be various degrees of incompetence of individuals and/or incompetence of management. The revised ISO 9001 appears to recognize this by placing emphasis on the responsibilities of management and requiring evidence that employee training has resulted in individuals being competent, or that they have achieved new competences as a result of their training (see clause 6.2.2).

Internal audit (ISO 9001, clause 8.2.2)

There is a mandatory procedure (see PC 103) on internal auditing that defines:

- the responsibilities and requirements for planning and conducting audits;

- how results will be reported;

- how records will be kept and maintained.

With ISO 9001, the main focus of internal auditing is on process diagrams, care plans and the resulting outcomes. For instance, auditors would be expected to follow a process diagram from the time a resident enquires about a home to the time that they enter a home, and in the period thereafter. In working through a first-level process, pauses in the steps forward will be inevitable and frequent. For instance, any attached notes will have to be checked, as will any lower-level processes. These, in turn, may lead to an examination of compliance with other documents associated with the processes.

An audit programme, or audit schedule, must be prepared that covers all the areas to be audited. Once all the first-level processes in a home have been clearly identified, all the audits associated with such processes can be planned. The schedule must identify the frequency of such audits based on the status and importance of various activities. The schedule of internal audits should be flexible, and changes will be inevitable as the results of earlier audits become available, when the need for an earlier re-audit might become apparent.

Auditing is both an art and a science. Internal auditing must be carried out by trained and competent auditors. Training can be conducted by the organization's own experienced auditors, or it can be done externally by attendance on approved courses. Any good auditor can conduct an internal audit in any circumstances. Less experienced auditors would benefit from the preparation of audit questions before an audit is conducted (see Chapter 9). The questions need not be rigidly adhered to. They can be regarded as starter questions that will lead on to further questioning, if an auditor feels that there is a need to pursue matters in greater detail.

A well designed nonconformity form and an observation report form included in procedure PC 103 are recommended for use during internal audits. The observation form is simpler and any observation made is stated merely to promote later discussions with all interested parties, with a view to improving the way in which processes proceed to their final conclusions.

The focus on processes will mean that internal audits are likely to take much more time and skill than would be the case if an auditor were merely checking for compliance with one or more, perhaps somewhat isolated, procedures. Auditing should be interesting and meaningful because of its direct link with the reasons for a home existing. Moreover, in discussions with auditees, it should provide opportunities for considering ways in which changes might be made to the major process and, of course, to the associated processes, so that a major process can be improved.

All employees of a home should view auditing in a positive light. Its purpose is to make things better for all concerned, but especially better for the residents. The impartial auditing process enables any shortcomings in a process to be highlighted and affords an excellent opportunity to make continuing improvements in the effectiveness of the quality management system. Any improvements will aid the overall efficiency of the home with consequential benefits to maintaining and, when possible, improving the quality of life for residents. Maximum benefits accrue from internal auditing when there is openness, integrity and responsibility.

The findings and follow-up actions arising from internal audits are a key item on the agenda of management review meetings, which includes the effectiveness of any corrective and preventive actions.

Monitoring and measurement of processes (ISO 9001, clause 8.2.3)

All first-level processes must be monitored as and when deemed necessary in such ways that the output of a first-level process will focus on an end result that is intended to achieve the maintenance of, and, whenever possible an improved, quality of life for residents. All monitoring is done with the intention of confirming the continuing ability of each first-level process to achieve the specified requirements at each stage of that process. In the event that requirements are not being met, a nonconformity should be raised on the nonconformity form referred to earlier in connection with internal audits.

Notes attached to process diagrams and any lower-level processes also need to be monitored in the same way. Notes and any lower-level processes do not necessarily impact directly on major processes. For instance, a failure to carry out a process might not prevent a first-level process from proceeding to the required output, i.e. maintenance of, and whenever possible an improvement in, the quality of life of a resident. One example of a lower-level process would be in connection with the calibration of equipment. If recalibration of equipment has not taken place at the scheduled time, it does not mean that the equipment was necessarily inaccurate at the time it was used in a first-level process. Nevertheless, a nonconformity must be raised when there is objective evidence that the calibration has not been done by the scheduled date.

Measurement and monitoring of product (ISO 9001, clause 8.2.4)

Measurements and monitoring of product (i.e. the maintenance of, and whenever possible improvement in, the quality of life of residents) must take place at appropriate stages of first-level processes to ensure that the planned care routine is being followed (see clause 7.1). Self-medication (see PD 103) is an example of an important process that must be adhered to for some residents, because the failure of a resident to take self-medication, or the correct amounts of medicine, will probably mean that the quality of life of the resident is unlikely to be maintained. Evidence of conformity with PD 103 must be documented (see clause 4.2.4). and such documentation is placed in the resident's file. This is but one example of processes that need to be monitored, because deviation from what has been planned for a resident will probably have a deleterious effect on the resident.

Control of nonconforming product (ISO 9001, clause 8.3)

The planned product output of a residential care home is always the same, namely, the maintenance of, and whenever possible improvement in, the quality of life of residents.

Any failure to maintain the quality of life for a resident might arise because what was planned for a particular resident was not carried out, or not carried out satisfactorily; or simply because, for reasons unknown at the time, a resident has not responded to the planned care as expected. If a resident is not responding to the planned care, the care manager would examine the resident's care plan and, perhaps after taking advice from professional staff outside the home, amend the care plan in accordance with advice received.

Other nonconformities in the home might not have a direct impact on the care of residents.

Nevertheless, these must also be addressed.

A mandatory procedure PC 104, Control of nonconforming product, ensures that all product and service nonconformities are addressed properly in a systematic manner.

Analysis of data (ISO 9001, clause 8.4)

A home has to determine what data, when collected, collated and analysed, can be used to demonstrate the suitability and effectiveness of its quality management system and show how such analyses can be used to achieve continual improvement in the effectiveness of the quality management system (see clause 8.5.1).

Data can be obtained from any relevant sources in addition to the four sources specifically named in the standard. These are:

(a)   the characteristics and trends of resident processes and resident outcomes, including opportunities for preventive action;

(b)   achievements in maintaining and, whenever possible, improving the quality of life of residents (see clause 7.2.1);

(c)   resident satisfaction (see clause 8.2.1);

(d)   the performance of suppliers.

Improvement (ISO 9001, clause 8.5)

Continual improvement (ISO 9001, clause 8.5.1)

The home must continually improve the effectiveness of its quality management system. This is an explicit requirement that is repeated many times in ISO 9001.

Planning and striving for continual improvements in the effectiveness of the quality management system is to be achieved through the use of the quality policy, quality objectives, internal auditing, analysis of data, corrective and preventive actions and through management reviews.

The requirement for continual improvement in the effectiveness of the quality management system means that a home should always be striving to make changes that will result in it doing things in better ways in the interests of efficiency and economy. In fact these are all the things that a good home should be doing in any case, irrespective of ISO 9001. Some of the changes in management of a home, new resources (more competent people and better physical resources), better monitoring and measurements during processes, better collection and analysis of data, and improved technology are initiatives that might result in continual improvements in the effectiveness of a quality management system.

Corrective action (ISO 9001, clause 8.5.2)

A home must take corrective action to eliminate the cause of nonconformities discovered in caring or associated processes, during internal audits, and in response to complaints from residents and their relatives or other interested parties.

One mandatory procedure, PC 105 Corrective action (arising from nonconformities and residents' complaints), is provided.

In some cases, such as death, corrective action clearly cannot be taken, but some kind of preventive action (see PC 106, Preventive action) might well prevent unnecessary deaths, or unnecessary suffering in the future, for other residents (see clause 8.5.3).

Some nonconformities might have little, if any, impact on the care of residents. These should be recorded in the same manner, but any corrective action might not be so urgent.

Nonconformities have been addressed in clause 8.3 and in procedure, PC 104.

Corrective actions and resident complaints

The information here relates to regulation 22 [3] and standard 16 [4].

There seems to be some doubt about what is meant by a resident complaint. A good guideline is that if anyone in a home feels that they should apologize to a resident, because the resident appears to be aggrieved by what has happened, or by what has not happened, then a complaint has been received. It may appear to be an unjustifiable complaint, but the resident evidently thinks otherwise, so it would be advisable to be cautious and to promise to investigate the complaint without delay.

There must be a full investigation and response to resident complaints, be they verbal or written complaints. All resident complaints should be logged and dealt with in a systematic manner as detailed in the mandatory procedure PC 105, Corrective action.

There is little difference in the ways in which nonconformities and complaints are dealt with, apart from the need for a quick response from the home in the case of the latter.

Management should look upon resident complaints in a positive manner. They should not be used to ostracize people. Complaints are an important management tool, whereby lessons can be learnt.

The absence of resident complaints must not lead to the assumption that all residents are entirely satisfied with a home. Some homes may not have a sufficiently accessible method of dealing with complaints. The introduction of a quality management system based on ISO 9001 will certainly ensure there is one. All complaints, not just the serious ones, must be systematically recorded and dealt with promptly.

Preventive action (ISO 9001, clause 8.5.3)

Preventive action is action taken to prevent something that has happened in the past (nonconformities, resident complaints) from taking place again in the future. Another important kind of preventive action is action taken to prevent something from happening in the future that has not happened so far. A mandatory procedure is required on preventive actions (see PC 106).

Any preventive actions taken must be appropriate to the impact of the problem that has arisen. For instance, what is considered to be a one-off occurrence (assuming no serious resident outcome has occurred) should not result in enormous expenditure to prevent its recurrence in the future. Similarly, a theoretical possibility of something occurring in the future might not justify considerable expense to reduce the probability of its happening. Thus, it might be decided in the case of a particular incident that no preventive action is to be taken.

Chapter 9:
Guideline audit questions

Introduction

These guideline audit questions can be used for internal auditing, i.e. by a care home carrying out it own audits, and for third-party audits conducted by an accredited certification body for the award of an ISO 9001 certificate.

In the earlier chapters of this book, reference has been made to the care homes regulations and to the national minimum standards that are now applicable to care homes. Where there is some correlation between the regulations and the standards and with ISO 9001, the audit questions have been printed in *italics*. For the convenience of care homes that are about to be inspected by a local authority and/or the Commission for Social Care and Inspection, the *italicized* audit questions might be used by the internal auditors of a care home as practice questions. The list does not purport to be comprehensive, but it will help care homes that are conducting internal audits to get used to asking the right questions of their colleagues. Care homes that are to be inspected by external organizations are not required to train their staff in the processes of auditing, but some practice could prove very useful.

To return to ISO 9001 quality management system auditing, as explained in the previous chapters, the revised standard focuses on the processes by which a care home meets the needs and expectations of residents, and thereby maintains and, whenever possible, improves the quality of life of residents. Example process diagrams are included in Chapter 3 to illustrate what can be achieved by using such process diagrams. A care home can introduce as many as it pleases. Process auditing means that the auditor is checking the sequential and interrelated steps from the beginning of a first-level process until the required output has been achieved. The interrelated steps might be notes attached to the stages in a process diagram or they might be lower-level processes, or both. Such process auditing, rather than compliance auditing, might prove to be more attractive and understandable to some, because it relates more easily to the step-by-step processes that are so important in the provision of first-class care for residents.

In spite of this emphasis on process auditing, there will still be a need for some compliance auditing. Compliance auditing will be necessary when checking on the stand-alone processes such as the calibration of instruments. Calibration of instruments might be a necessary requirement but, in general, the failure to calibrate a device on a certain date will not, and should not, stop a main process from continuing as planned.

This chapter includes a comprehensive list of typical audit questions that address the requirements of ISO 9001 and the Commission for Social Care and Inspection. The reader, when process auditing, can then select the relevant questions when following a specific audit trail through a first-level process, pausing as necessary, when interacting processes intervene, until the intended output has been achieved. Compliance auditing is much more straightforward and likely to be less time consuming, but the specific questions listed should also be helpful.

Another approach to be recommended to inexperienced auditors is to concentrate on particular clauses of the standard. Concentrate on them until you are absolutely certain you understand them individually and as a group. Write down your own ideas on how to address them. Often, there is more than one way. Ask colleagues and friends how they would address them and then, if possible, see how they have been addressed by experts in the field. Out of such endeavours you will become fully familiar with the requirements of the standard. You will soon know how to address requirements and, after carrying out one or two process audits and perhaps several compliance audits that involve the clauses in question, you will find that you will only occasionally have to refer to the relevant audit questions, or to the standard itself. Moreover, if your auditing decisions are ever challenged you will be in a strong position to answer any criticisms.

Auditors need to have many attributes. Auditing is not just about having a list of possible questions. Newcomers to auditing might benefit from studying *ISO 9000 Quality Systems Auditing* [5].

Quality management system (ISO 9001, clause 4)

General requirements (ISO 9001, clause 4.1)

I understand that you have established a quality management system?
Has it been fully implemented?
How is it maintained?

What do you understand by the requirement that the care home must continually improve the effectiveness of your quality management system?

Please identify and describe the care home's major (or first-level) processes.
Please show me examples of such processes in connection with:

- choosing a care home;

- care plans;

- medication;

- resident complaints.

Do you use lower-level processes?
Can you please show me any examples of lower-level processes?

Please show me how the lower-level processes interrelate with the first-level processes at the appropriate times and that they all function as planned.

What criteria and methods are used to ensure that the operation and control of first-level and lower-level processes are effective?

How do you ensure the availability of appropriate resources?

How do you ensure that appropriate documentation/information is always readily available to support the operation and monitoring of the processes?

What monitoring and measurements take place during the processes, followed by analyses, to ensure that planned results are achieved?

Have such monitoring, measurements and analyses ever resulted in continual improvements being made in the processes?
Can you please give me examples?

Are any processes outsourced that could affect the planned maintenance and, if possible, improvement in the quality of life of residents?
Are outsourced processes clearly identified in the quality management system?
How are outsourced processes controlled?
Please can I see examples of controlled outsourcing?

Documentation requirements (ISO 9001, clause 4.2)

General (ISO 9001, clause 4.2.1)

Please show me the documentation on which the quality management system is based.
Is it partly or wholly on intranet?
If it is on intranet who has the read and write facility?

How many hard copies of the quality manual are there?
Can I please see several such copies?
Are they uniquely identified?
What are their issue numbers?
What are the dates on the quality manual?

Can I please see your quality policy statement?
Is the quality policy statement a stand-alone document?
Does it have an issue number?
Is it dated?
Who has signed it?
How are changes in the quality policy controlled?
If changes have been made, how would I know that I was looking at the latest version?
How many copies have been issued?
How does the care home make the quality policy known to all members of staff?
Are the quality policy documents controlled documents?

Can I please see a list of your quality objectives?
Who decides what the quality objectives should be?
Are the quality objectives issued to all staff as a stand-alone document?
Does the quality objectives document have an issue number?
Is the document dated?

Who has signed it?

Quality objectives will be changed from time to time. How do I know that I am looking at the latest list?

How does the care home make the quality objectives known to all members of staff?

Please show me the following mandatory procedures:

> control of documents;

> control of records;

> internal audit;

> control of nonconforming product;

> corrective action;

> preventive action.

These will be examined in detail at appropriate times during an audit.

How are the procedures controlled?

Who has copies of these procedures?

Do you have a list of recipients?

Are the procedures issued against documentation?

If you have to make a change to one page in a procedure (or any other document) how would you go about it?

If you had to make a significant change to a controlled document, how would you go about it?

Please show me any other documentation (process diagrams, procedures, policies, work instructions, forms) that are necessary for control of the quality management system.

Please show me any other documentation (procedures, flow diagrams, work instructions, forms, internal documents) that is being used in the care home to ensure effective planning, operation and control of all the first-level processes and any lower-level processes.

Are notes attached to any of the stages in the processes?

Please show me an example.

Likewise, can you show me a lower-level process diagram?

Am I correct in saying that you have established records that provide objective evidence of conformity to requirements and the effective operation of your quality management system?

Do you have a comprehensive list of such records?

Can I see samples of a number of such records now please?

(I will ask to see other records as and when deemed appropriate.)

Quality manual (ISO 9001, clause 4.2.2)

> Does the quality manual include the scope of the quality management system?
> Please may I see it?
>
> Have all the requirements of the standard been addressed?
> If not, are the exclusions from clause 7 recorded in the quality manual?
> Have you justified in the quality manual the reasons for the exclusions?
> Please will you go through the arguments for such exclusions now?
>
> Does the quality manual include a description of the sequence and interaction of all the major processes?
> Please show me how you have achieved this.
>
> Does the quality manual make reference to procedures at appropriate points in the text?
> Please show me examples.
> Does the quality manual include procedures, or are they compiled separately?
> If procedures are filed separately from the quality manual, are procedures listed in the quality manual?

Control of documents (ISO 9001, clause 4.2.3)

> The control of documents procedure must explain how the quality management system documents are controlled. The procedure, together with the quality manual, must answer the following questions.
>
> Who finally approves documents (the quality manual, process diagrams, procedures, protocols, work instructions and forms) for adequacy, before they are allowed to become part of the quality management system?
> Please show me evidence of this.
>
> How are documents readily identifiable?
> Do they have unique reference letters and/or numbers?
> How does the care home ensure that all documents are readily available?
> How does the care home ensure that all documents remain legible?
>
> What arrangements are in place for reviewing, updating as necessary, and re-approving such documents prior to their being reissued?
>
> How is the revision status of a document, or part of a document, identified?
> Please show me examples.
> How are changes in a document identified?
> Please show me examples.
>
> How does the management representative, or another named person, ensure that relevant versions of applicable documents are always available at points of use or application?
> Please show me an example.
>
> How are documents of external origin (e.g. standards, codes of practice and forms) controlled to ensure that only the latest issues of such documents can be used?
> Is there a master list of external documents?

What happens to superseded documents?

What precautions are taken to prevent unintended use of obsolete documents?

Are they returned to the management representative, or another person, on receipt of an updated document, or when a document is no longer applicable?

Is one copy, clearly marked 'superseded', filed separately and retained for knowledge preservation purposes?

Control of records (ISO 9001, clause 4.2.4)

The control of records procedure must explain how the quality management system records are controlled. The procedure, together with the quality manual, must answer the following questions.

Does it include a list of records that have to be kept for purposes of the ISO 9001: 2000?

Are records always clearly identifiable?
Please show me examples.

Are all records stored carefully?
Can I please see how they are stored?

Can all records be retrieved easily?
How, for instance, can I retrieve...?

Are all records protected from possible damage?
Please show me examples of protection,

Are all records legible and do they remain legible?
Please can I see some of your older records?

Have retention times of different records been defined?
Please give examples and explain any different requirements.

Who has the authority to dispose of records?
Can you give me an example of disposal and the authority for such disposal?

Management responsibility (ISO 9001, clause 5)

Management commitment (ISO 9001, clause 5.1)

These questions would be addressed to the registered person.

I have already spent some time seeking objective evidence about your quality management system based on the ISO 9001: 2000. I am impressed (or unimpressed) by what I have found so far during the audit. Everyone has been most courteous and helpful (or, say, courteous, but reluctantly helpful or whatever is appropriate).
Would you kindly let them know what I feel?

The ISO 9001 makes it clear that top management, in your case, yourself, has to be actively involved in the quality management system of the care home. All six clauses in clause 5 begin: 'Top management shall…'

I have asked to spend a little time with you, because I hope you will be able to convince me of your commitment to the development and implementation of your quality management system and your commitment to continual improvement in the effectiveness of the quality management system of your care home. With these points in mind, I would like to ask you a few questions.

I have read your quality policy, signed by you, and dated dd/mm/yy.
What do you think about having to provide a quality policy statement for your care home?

What are your views on having to establish quality objectives?

Do you chair the management review meetings?
Are they particularly enlightening from a management point of view?

Who is responsible for ensuring that adequate resources are available for the development, implementation and continual improvement of the quality management system?

How do you ensure that all employees are aware of the need to strive at all times to maintain and, when possible, improve the quality of life of all residents?

At the end of the interview an auditor must make a judgement as to whether top management is committed to the development, implementation and continual improvement in the effectiveness of the quality management system.

The final judgement will be influenced to some extent by any objective evidence obtained earlier and later in the audit. This explains the importance of not interviewing top management at the beginning of an audit.

Subjective and objective evidence

There are four possibilities.

1. Subjective evidence and objective evidence good.

If the somewhat subjective evidence collected from the discussion with the registered person is good and the objective evidence is good, the commitment of top management to the quality management system would appear to be satisfactory.

2. Subjective evidence good and objective evidence poor.

If the subjective evidence is good, but the objective evidence is poor, then top management has evidently failed to develop and implement its quality management system satisfactorily.

3. Subjective evidence bad/poor and objective evidence good.

If the subjective evidence is bad, or poor, and the objective evidence collected is good, this would suggest that the quality management system is functioning satisfactory in spite of the lack of enthusiastic commitment of top management.

4. Subjective evidence bad/poor and objective evidence poor.

If the subjective evidence is bad or poor and the objective evidence collected is also poor, it can be safely assumed that the quality management system is operating under most unsatisfactory conditions with little commitment of top management.

In both of the circumstances in which the subjective evidence suggests lack of top management commitment, an auditor would be wise to refrain from commenting until the closing meeting of the audit. By that time they might have collected other damaging objective evidence to support earlier impressions of the lack of commitment of top management.

Customer focus (ISO 9001, clause 5.2)

One of the requirements in the standard is to ensure that the needs and expectations of customers, in this case residents, are determined and are then converted into resident requirements, so that through the first-level processes of the care home it is evident that the care home is striving at all times and with all residents to maintain and, whenever possible, improve their quality of life.

How does the care home address the following needs of residents:

- privacy?
- common courtesies?
- cleanliness at all times and in all places?
- good food?

What else does the care home do to ensure that the needs and expectations of residents are addressed at all times?

Quality policy (ISO 9001, clause 5.3)

I have read carefully your quality policy statement signed by you (or whoever) and date dd/mm/yy. It seems appropriate for your kind of care home and is positive in every respect.

How do you ensure that people at all levels in your care home know about the quality policy and understand what it means?

How do you ensure that the quality policy is reviewed for its continuing suitability?

I note the commitment of top management to comply with the requirements of the ISO 9001: 2000.
Can you give me one or more examples in which the requirements of the standard have resulted in changes in the ways in which the care home operates?

I note your commitment to improve continually the effectiveness of the quality management system.
What do you understand by this statement?
How do you go about ensuring that this happens?

Planning (ISO 9001, clause 5.4)

Quality objectives (ISO 9001, clause 5.4.1)

How does the care home decide on measurable quality objectives?

Are they set for higher levels of management/senior staff as well as for less senior staff or at department level?

Is there a framework for establishing and reviewing quality objectives in a systematic manner?
Please explain and show me examples.

Are all of the quality objectives compatible with the quality policy statement?

Quality management system planning (ISO 9001, clause 5.4.2)

When planning the quality management system were the general requirements of the system addressed (see clause 4.1), as well as the quality objectives (see clause 5.4.1)?

When changes to the quality management system are planned and implemented, who is responsible for ensuring that the integrity of the quality management system is maintained? Can you please show me an example of such a change?

Responsibility, authority and communication (ISO 9001, clause 5.5)

Responsibility and authority (ISO 9001, clause 5.5.1)

How do you ensure that responsibilities and authorities are defined and communicated within the care home?

Does the care home have an organization chart?
Please may I see it?

If the organization chart is not in general circulation, how are employees expected to know who is responsible for what?

If there are no names, or very few names, on the care home chart, how do individuals know who reports to whom?

Are the responsibilities and authorities of individuals clearly specified?
Please show me examples.

Management representative (ISO 9001, clause 5.5.2)

Has management appointed a management representative (or quality manager)?

Have their responsibilities and authority been defined?
May I see please?

How does management ensure that the responsibilities and authority of the management representative for establishing, implementing and maintaining the quality management system are known to all members of staff?

What measures have been taken by management to ensure that staff members know that the management representative has a direct line of responsibility to you?
May I please see your latest care home organization chart again?

To whom does the management representative report on the performance of the quality management system?
Please show me examples of such reporting.

To whom does the management representative report on the need for any changes to be made for improvement of the quality management system?
Can you show me some examples?

How does the management representative ensure the promotion of awareness of resident requirements throughout the care home?
(The prime requirement is to maintain, and, whenever possible, improve the quality of life for all residents. Secondary requirements are: privacy; common courtesies at all times; cleanliness at all times and in all places; and good food. Everyone should have their parts to play in achieving these requirements.)
Can you please show me examples of how such desirable requirements are promoted?

What other responsibilities, if any, does your management representative have?

Is the management representative responsible for liaison with external parties, e.g. certification bodies?
If not, who is responsible for such activities and what arrangements are there to ensure that the management representative is kept fully informed of such developments?

Internal communication (ISO 9001, clause 5.5.3)

How do you ensure that appropriate communication processes are established within your care home?

How do you ensure that communication takes place within your care home regarding the effectiveness of the quality management system?

Management review (ISO 9001, clause 5.6)

General (ISO 9001, clause 5.6.1)

What arrangements are in place for top management to review the quality management system to ensure its continuing suitability, adequacy and effectiveness?

What are the planned intervals between such meetings?
Please show me that the planned intervals between management review meetings have been kept.

Have the reviews of the quality management system shown that it continues to be suitable, adequate and effective for the care home?

Have such reviews resulted in opportunities for changes to be made that have resulted in continual improvement in the effectiveness of the quality management system?
Please show me one example of such continual improvement.

The reviews provide opportunities for changes to be made to the quality policy. Have any such changes been made?

Have the reviews resulted in the need for changes to quality objectives?
Can you show me an example of such a change?

Are records kept of management review meetings (see clause 4.2.4)?
Please may I see the records of the last few management review meetings?

Review input (ISO 9001, clause 5.6.2)

Do you have a standard agenda for your management review meetings?

As a minimum, does it include the following:

(a)   follow-up actions from earlier management reviews?

(b)   the results of audits (both internal and any external)?

(c)   improvements in processes (resident pathways)?

(d)   successes in maintaining and, whenever possible, improving the quality of life for residents?

(e)   failures to maintain, and, whenever might have been possible, to improve the quality of life for residents because of adverse events and 'near misses'?

(f)   status of corrective and preventive actions?

(g)   resident feedback (resident complaints and answers to questionnaires on resident satisfaction)?

(h)   recommendations for improvement in the effectiveness of the quality management system?

(i)   any changes, whatever their origin or nature, that could have a bearing on the quality management system?

Review output (ISO 9001, clause 5.6.3)

Can you give me examples of decisions and actions decided at management review meetings that have resulted in:

(a)   improvement in the effectiveness of the quality management system and its processes?

(b)   improvements in quality of life for residents?

(c)   the need for more resources?

Do you have a standard agenda for a management review meeting?
Please may I see one?

Resource management (ISO 9001, clause 6)

Provision of resources (ISO 9001, clause 6.1)

Who is responsible for determining and providing resources needed for implementation and maintenance of the quality management system?
Can I please see an example of this?

What effort is given to determining and providing resources that will result in continual improvement in the effectiveness of the quality management system?

Does the home determine and provide the resources needed to enhance resident satisfaction by:
*   helping care staff to maintain and, whenever possible, improve the quality of life of residents?
*   helping other staff to provide all the other services in connection with residential care?
Please show me at least one example in each category.

Human resources (ISO 9001, clause 6.2)

How do you ensure that caring staff whose prime duties and responsibilities are to maintain and, whenever possible, improve the quality of lives of residents, and other staff who provide all the other services in connection with resident care, are competent for such tasks on the basis of their relevant education, training, skills and experience?
Can you give me a few examples?

General (ISO 9001, clause 6.2.1)

Competence, awareness and training (ISO 9001, clause 6.2.2)

Are competency needs defined for caring staff who are responsible for the maintenance and, whenever possible, improvement in the quality of life for residents and for all the other staff who are responsible for providing other services in connection with resident care?
Please show me several examples for caring staff and other staff.

How does the home arrange training, where necessary, or other actions, to achieve the defined competences in those cases in which competency has been found wanting? Can you please show me evidence of this?

How is in-house training (and any external training) evaluated? Please can I see examples?

How do you ensure that all employees are made aware of the relevance and importance of their activities and how each one contributes to the achievement of quality objectives? How do you ensure that any new employees are suitably briefed on this matter? Please show me examples.

How do you maintain appropriate records of all staff on education, training, skills and experience (see clause 4.2.4)? Please may I choose, at random, some training records for examination? Also, specifically, may I see the training record(s) of your internal auditor(s)? How do you ensure that all records are kept up to date?

Infrastructure (ISO 9001, clause 6.3)

If a home is to continue to maintain and, whenever possible, improve the quality of life for residents, and ensure that other staff provide a satisfactory service in connection with resident care, then management has to determine, provide and maintain an appropriate infrastructure.

Who is responsible for providing and maintaining an appropriate infrastructure? In particular, who is responsible for buildings? Who is responsible for toilets? Please show me examples.

Who makes decisions on any support services that are necessary for carers who are striving to maintain and, whenever possible, improve the quality of life of residents? Please give examples.

What support services are outsourced? Who is responsible for ensuring that outsourced services are of the required standard? Please show me examples.

Work environment (ISO 9001, clause 6.4)

How does management determine, provide and manage the human and physical factors of the work environment that are necessary for all staff who are trying to maintain and, whenever possible, improve the quality of life of residents, and for staff that provide other services in connection with resident care?

Do these include:

*   safety of individuals?
*   ergonomics of working?
*   appropriate lighting levels?

> - appropriate temperature and humidity controls?
> - acceptable noise levels?
> - acceptable levels of cleanliness and hygiene?
> - minimum pollution levels?
> - appropriate protective equipment?
>
> Which of these are covered by legislation, regulations or codes of practice?
>
> What controls are in place to ensure that the planned work environments are maintained?

Product realization (ISO 9001, clause 7)

Planning of product realization (ISO 9001, clause 7.1)

> Any care plan for a resident has one prime objective: to maintain and, whenever possible, to improve the quality of life of residents. Management has the responsibility of ensuring that carers and all the support services needed in connection with the care of residents are provided in a timely and efficient manner.
>
> Can I please see several such quality plans?
>
> Have all the processes been clearly identified (first-level processes; lower-level processes, etc.)?
> Have the sequence and interaction of these processes been made clear?
>
> Have the criteria and methods been determined to ensure that processes proceed to their planned outputs, i.e. they contribute in one way or another to maintaining and, whenever possible, improving the quality of life of residents in an effective manner?
>
> Who ensures that suitable resources are provided with the aim of maintaining, and whenever possible, improving the quality of lives of residents?
>
> Do the planned processes indicate where suitable documentation has to be made available in order that the processes can proceed in an effective manner?
>
> Do the planned processes show what monitoring and measurements have to be made, and where and when?
>
> Are all the tests that residents have to undergo, if any, clearly identified?
>
> If outsourced products or services are used by staff in connection with resident care, how is the outsourcing adequately controlled?
>
> Do any resident treatment plans identify what records are to be kept and maintained as residents make progress towards achieving an improved quality of life?

Customer-related processes (ISO 9001, clause 7.2)

The needs of residents are paramount. This is summarized by the requirement to maintain and, whenever possible, improve the quality of life of residents.

Long-term care of residents

Is there a document entitled 'statement of purpose'?
Please may I see it?
Does it include the aims and objectives for the care home?
Does it give in detail the facilities and services provided by the care home?

Is there a resident's guide for the care home?
Please may I see it?
Does the guide include a summary of the statement of purpose of the care home?
If not, is the guide always accompanied by the statement of purpose document?

Does the guide describe the accommodation available for a specified number of residents?
Does it state how many of the rooms are en-suite?
Does it state what public rooms are available: lounges, dining rooms, etc?

Does the guide explain the staffing arrangements?
What is the staff/resident ratio?

Does it explain how resident's complaints are dealt with?
Does it state that complaints can also be submitted to the Commission for Social Care and Inspection?
Does it give the address and telephone number of the Commission for Social Care and Inspection?

Does it include results of a recent resident satisfaction survey?

Does the guide include the latest inspection report from the Commission for Social Care and Inspection?

Have any changes been made to either the statement of purpose document or to the resident's guide document?
When were these changes made?
Was the Commission for Social Care and Inspection advised of the changes within 28 days of the changes being made?
Please show me any relevant correspondence on these matters.

Can you show me the correspondence relating to the last three cases in which there have been further enquiries about possible take-up of residence after the documentation has been sent to potential residents?

Do you have a process diagram that shows the sequence of steps to be followed by the care home in response to an enquiry about possible residence in the care home?
Please may I see it?

Who is responsible for compiling a record of the health needs of a potential resident?

Can we follow through the three cases referred to earlier?

Please show me, if possible, a case in which the needs of a prospective resident could not be met.

Short-term care of residents

Does the care home admit short-term care residents?

Please show me documentation for such a case.

In what way does the process of admission to the care home differ in the case of a short-term stay resident?

Emergency admissions

Does the care home accept emergency admissions?

Please show me the documentation for such a case.

In what way does the process of admission to the care home differ in the case of an emergency admission?

Determination of requirements related to the product (ISO 9001, clause 7.2.1)

Review of requirements related to the product (ISO 9001, clause 7.2.2)

Who is responsible for reviewing that the needs of a potential resident can be met?
Can I please see documented evidence of such reviews?

Do such reviews confirm that the needs of a potential resident have been adequately defined?
Have all requirements differing from those initially expressed been resolved?
Does the review show that the care home is able to meet the newly defined requirements?
Please may I see several contracts prepared after such reviews have been completed?

Customer communication (ISO 9001, clause 7.2.3)

What arrangements are in place to ensure that there are effective channels of communication between the home and its residents, or their nominees on all matters?
Is this documented? Please show me examples with residents and with their nominees.

How does the care home respond to feedback from residents:
* verbal feedback?
* written feedback?

Design and development (ISO 9001, clause 7.3)

This clause has been justifiably excluded.

Purchasing (ISO 9001, clause 7.4)

Purchasing process (ISO 9001, clause 7.4.1)

What kinds of controls are exercised by the care home over suppliers and subcontractors that can have a bearing on the maintenance and, whenever possible, improvement in the quality of the life of residents?

What criteria are used for their selection?
Are evaluations carried out periodically?
If so, is this done at defined intervals?

Are records of the results of all evaluations kept and maintained as records?
Can I please see such records?

Can I please see any records of re-evaluations that have become necessary because of unsatisfactory product or poor service?

Has the introduction of purchasing controls resulted in a reduction in the number of suppliers and subcontractors, with consequential savings in administration?

Purchasing information (ISO 9001, clause 7.4.2)

Could I please see a few purchasing orders?

How are orders reviewed and approved to ensure the adequacy of specified purchase requirements before the orders are despatched?
Please show me examples.

Verification of purchased product (ISO 9001, clause 7.4.3)

Is any purchased product examined before the time of its use?
If only certain products are examined before use, what criteria are used to determine what shall be examined on receipt?

In the case of a new supplier, does the care home impose strict verification processes?
Are the strict verification processes agreed in advance and implemented on receipt of goods?
Please show me an example.

Production and service provision (ISO 9001, clause 7.5)

Control of production and service provision (ISO 9001, clause 7.5.1)

What evidence is there that the care home provides the residential care as planned, under controlled conditions?

Care plans

Please may I see your process diagram in connection with care plans?

Please can I see your care plans for three residents?
Have they been approved by residents?
Have the residents signed the care plans indicating their approval?
Are the care plans dated?

Is there a systematic review of all care plans?
Please show me examples of such reviews.
Please show me three care plans that have been changed as a result of the systematic review process.
Please show me evidence that when changes to care plans are being considered, the proposed changes are discussed with residents and/or relatives before the care plans are changed.
Are all revised care plans dated?
Have all revised care plans been approved and signed by residents and/or relatives?

Are all care plans systematically filed in a secure place?
Can a resident always have access to their own care plan?

Resident's file

Do all residents have their own file, systematically filed in a secure place?

Does it contain all the relevant information about a resident?
Please may I see such files, chosen at random?

What documentation is in place for this resident?

What monitoring and measuring devices, if any, are being used?

Health of residents

Does the care home have any procedures that give guidance to carers on how they should deal with the more common health problems in elderly residents? For example, is there a procedure on incontinence?

Are all care staff aware that whenever there is a health problem of an unusual nature the care manager must be informed without delay?
How are staff made aware of this?

Medication

Is there a comprehensive procedure in place dealing with all aspects of medication: for the receipt, records, storage, handling, administration and disposal of drugs?

Is there a process diagram on medication?

Does the care home abide by all regulations, guidelines, etc, in connection with drugs?
What external documents do you have as reference documents?

What arrangements are made to ensure that drugs are stored at the right temperature?
Are records kept on the temperature of drug refrigerators?
How do you know that the thermometers are accurate?

Are care staff well trained and accredited in their basic knowledge of drugs?
Could I see evidence of such training and accreditation for several carers chosen at random?

Does the procedure on medication make it clear when a carer should seek guidance and help when a resident's condition deteriorates, possibly because of a drug-related problem?

Are residents assessed before they are allowed to take their own drugs?
Where is it documented as to who can make such assessments?
Please let me see three documented assessments, chosen at random.

When self-medication has been agreed, what precautions are in place for the safe and proper use of drugs?
How are the drugs supplied to a resident and in what quantities?
Are blister packs or dossette boxes used?
Are the drugs held securely in locked cupboards in residents' rooms?
Do the carers for such residents have access to the locked cupboards?
Do carers keep a record of the drugs taken by residents?

When residents are not allowed to self-medicate, who has the responsibility to administer drugs? Is this carefully documented?

What additional safeguards are in place for the delivery, safety, storage, administration and documentation of controlled drugs?

Who has the authority to administer controlled drugs?
Does administration of a controlled drug have to be witnessed?
Please show me documentary evidence.
Can I please see your controlled drugs register?

Do care staff receive any training in connection with controlled drugs?
Please can I see information and records on such training?

Does the registered person seek the advice of a pharmacist from time to time?

What happens to unused drugs when a resident dies?

Social contacts and activities

Meals and mealtimes

Are the kinds of meals for residents individually assessed according to requirements?
Please can I see the records on a number of assessments, selected at random?

Who ensures that residents have a varied, appealing, wholesome and nutritious diet?
Is food, including liquefied meals, presented in a manner that is attractive and appealing in terms of texture, flavour and appearance, in order to maintain appetite and nutrition?

Is there a menu for each meal that is changed regularly offering a choice of meals in a suitable format that is given to and, if necessary, read and explained to residents?

When advised by health care and dietary staff, are special therapeutic diets/feeds provided, including any requirements for calcium and vitamin D?

Are religious, cultural and dietary needs catered for as agreed prior to admission on special occasions as laid down in a resident's care plan?

Are residents allowed to eat their meals over whatever period of time they choose?

If residents need help in eating their food will assistance be given in a discreet and sensitive manner?

May I speak to residents on this point?

Are residents offered three meals each day at intervals not exceeding five hours?
Is at least one meal a cooked one?

Is a snack meal offered in the evening?
Does the interval between the snack meal and breakfast the following morning exceed 12 hours?

Are hot and cold drinks and snacks available at all times?

Are all meals provided in a congenial setting and at various times?

Autonomy and choice

Can residents bring personal possessions into the care home, subject to agreement prior to taking up residence?

Can residents examine their own records in the care home in accord with the Data Protection Act 1998?

Can residents make contacts with external agents and bodies?
Could I please ask a few residents about these points?

Does the care home make it known that it is able to put residents in touch with outside bodies if a resident or the families need confidential advice?

Daily life in the care home

Does daily life in the care home suit residents' expectations, preferences and capabilities?
May I speak, in private, to several residents on this point?

Are the in-house activities that are made available generally acceptable?
Do the planned activities include leisure, social and cultural activities?
Do the planned activities promote personal and social relationships?
Is provision made for any religious observances that might be desired for residents?
May I speak, in private, to several other residents on this point?

Are the interests of residents recorded in their individual files?
Does the care home attempt to enable residents to pursue such interests?
Please can I see several files and speak to the corresponding residents?

Are residents with disabilities encouraged to make the most of the opportunities available?
Can you introduce me to a resident with some sort of disability, e.g. impairment of vision or hearing?

How are planned activities in the care home publicized?
Can you show me an example?

Community activities

Are residents encouraged to have visitors, in particular, family and friends or from the community?
Can such people be seen privately?

Are the wishes of residents taken into account when visits are being arranged by local community groups and/or volunteers?

Please show me an example of a visit arranged in the last month with the consent of residents.

Privacy and dignity

Are residents made to feel that their privacy and dignity remain paramount at all times?

For example:
- *in personal care?*
- *in relation to access to their own room?*
- *during medical examinations?*
- *during private consultations?*
- *during discussions with and examinations by health and social care professionals?*
- *during discussions with legal and financial advisers?*
- *when receiving visitors: family, relatives and friends?*
- *during private telephone conversations?*

Is all mail given to residents unopened?

Are residents encouraged to wear their own clothes?

Are terms of address formal, friendly and respectful?
If a resident asks to be called by a first name, or even a nickname, is such a request granted and made known to other staff and, with the resident's permission, to other residents?

If a resident occupies a shared room, is suitable screening provided to ensure that privacy is not compromised when personal care, medical examinations, etc. are being given?

I would like to speak to a number of residents on these matters of privacy and dignity.

Dying and death

Is there a process diagram in place for dying and death?

Are all staff trained to talk sensitively and act appropriately when the death of a resident occurs? Can you provide evidence of such training?

Immediately before the death of a resident are the following conditions observed:

(a) *Is privacy and dignity maintained at all times and in all respects?*
(b) *Are the wishes of a dying person addressed as far as is possible?*
(c) *Is a dying person made as comfortable as possible?*
(d) *Is pain relief administered?*
(e) *Is a dying person allowed to continue to live in their room, surrounded by familiar objects?*
(f) *Are the wishes immediately prior to and after death established and documented, whenever possible, perhaps with the help of relatives and friends?*
(g) *Are care home staff and other residents encouraged to give support?*
(h) *Is professional help in dealing with the dying and death proffered?*
(i) *Can relatives and friends stay with the dying resident for as long as they wish?*

Immediately after death of a resident are the following conditions observed:

(a) *Is time allowed for family and friends to pay their last respects?*
(b) *Is the body of the resident handled in a dignified manner?*
(c) *Can bereavement counselling be provided, if required?*

Validation of processes for production and service provision (ISO 9001, clause 7.5.2)

This clause applies to those processes where the resulting outcome cannot be directly validated.

Does the care home have any processes, e.g. sterilization of instruments, for which only indirect validation is possible?

If this is the case any indirect validation must demonstrate the ability of the processes to achieve planned results. For instance:

- Have criteria been defined for review and approval of any such processes?
- Has the equipment used been approved by a recognized authority?
- Have personnel using the equipment been proved to be competent in the use of the equipment by a recognized authority?
- Are specific methods and procedures being used that have been approved by recognized bodies?
- Are appropriate records kept and maintained in this connection?
- Whenever planned outcome is evidently not being achieved, does re-validation take place following appropriate changes to equipment, materials or staff?

Identification and traceability (ISO 9001, clause 7.5.3)

Identification

Are residents are formally identified by their full names?
Are birth certificates, or a copy of birth certificates, kept in the files of residents?

Traceability

It is essential that full traceability is established on drugs and controlled drugs (see 'Medication' above).

Does the care home use traceability in any other ways, e.g. on outsourcing of services such as a cleaning service?

Customer property (ISO 9001, clause 7.5.4)

How does the care home ensure that due care is exercised with residents' property?
Does this include any money given to the care home for safe-keeping?
What records are kept in this respect?
Please may I see the records for two residents?

Are any confidential documents kept for residents?
Please may I see such records?

If any property of a resident is lost or damaged, is this made known to the resident?
May I please see any documents in this respect?

Please can I speak privately to some residents on these matters?

Preservation of product (ISO 9001, clause 7.5.5)

The product of a care home has been defined as the maintenance and, whenever possible, improvement in the quality of life of residents.

Are you confident that every effort is made to ensure that this defined output is being sought at all times?
Please may I speak to a number of residents selected at random on this point?

Identification

Have there been any circumstances in which the normal names of residents have not been used for formal identification purposes?

Handling

How does the care home ensure that all residents are handled carefully so that residents and staff are not injured, whilst residents are being lifted or handled in any way?

Has the care home issued guidelines on how to handle residents safely at all times? Please may I see the guidelines?

Packaging

Not applicable.

Storage

Not applicable.

Protection

How does the care home provide protection for its residents from malicious damage, assault, etc. whilst they are within the confines of the care home?

Preservation

The planned product of a care home is the maintenance and, whenever possible, improvement in the quality of life of residents. How does management ensure that staff members are repeatedly reminded of this objective?

Delivery

How does the care home ensure that when a resident has to move to another room within the confines of the care home; or is transferred to another care home; or is transferred to other places for treatment, such as a dental surgery, that great care is exercised to ensure that such moves are carried out in a safe manner?
Can you show me several such examples?
Can I please speak to several residents on this point?

Control of monitoring and measuring devices (ISO 9001, clause 7.6)

Do you have any equipment in the care home whose temperature needs to be measured? Are there any limitations placed on such temperatures, for both maximum and minimum temperatures?

How do you ensure that the equipment has remained within the acceptable range?

How do you know that the temperature measurements are within acceptable limits of accuracy?

What records are kept on temperature measurements?
Please may I see examples?

Is the accuracy of any thermometers used for such purposes checked?
How?

Is a secondary standard used to check the accuracy of the thermometers?
Has it been calibrated by a calibration laboratory accredited by the United Kingdom Accreditation Service?

Measurement, analysis and improvement (ISO 9001, clause 8)

General (ISO 9001, clause 8.1)

There is a requirement on the care home to plan and implement:

* any monitoring and measurement processes;
* analysis processes (with explanations of the methods used);
* the improvement processes;

in order:

* to ensure conformity of the quality management system to the requirements of ISO 9001;
* to improve continually the effectiveness of the quality management system;
* to demonstrate a requirement to maintain and, whenever possible, improve the quality of life of residents.

Do you feel confident that the care home has addressed these issues in general?
The more specific requirements and associated requirements are addressed in clause 8.2.

Monitoring and measurement (ISO 9001, clause 8.2)

Customer satisfaction (ISO 9001, clause 8.2.1)

Does the care home monitor resident satisfaction?

What methods are used to obtain information relating to resident perceptions on whether the care home has maintained and, whenever possible, improved the quality of life of residents?

How is the information obtained used to determine such resident perceptions?

Can I please see the latest findings?
Are they more satisfactory than earlier findings?

Does the home believe that it has maintained and, when possible, improved the quality of life for residents?

Internal audit (ISO 9001, clause 8.2.2)

What do you think is the purpose of internal audits?
Are they to determine whether the quality management system conforms to the requirements of the standard?
Are they to determine whether the quality management system has been effectively implemented and is being maintained?
Are they to confirm that the care home is conforming to any planned arrangements, e.g. as specified in clause 7.1?

Does the mandatory procedure, internal audits, explain how internal audits are controlled?

The procedure, together with the quality manual, must answer the following questions:

- Are the responsibilities and requirements for planning and conducting audits clearly stated?
- Are the methods of reporting results clearly defined?
- Does the procedure make clear how records will be kept and maintained?

May I please see your audit programme?
Has consideration been given to the status and importance of the activities and areas to be audited, as well as to the results of previous audits?
Does anyone audit their own work?

Please show me evidence that auditors have been trained.

Please may I see the records of a few internal audits?

How does management ensure that timely corrective action is taken on nonconformities and any observations found during the audit?
Please show me a few examples.

How is verification of any corrective and preventive actions achieved?

How are results recorded and reported to management?

Measurement and monitoring of processes (ISO 9001, clause 8.2.3)

How are all first-level and any lower-level processes monitored as and when deemed necessary, so that the quality of life of the residents is maintained and, whenever possible, improved?
Can you show me one example of monitoring undertaken for this purpose?

If the monitoring does not confirm that the planned requirements are being followed, how is this dealt with?
Can you please show me any specific examples of any such nonconformities that have been found?

Monitoring and measurement of product (ISO 9001, clause 8.2.4)

The overall plan for all residents is that their quality of life should be maintained and, whenever possible, improved. How is this objective monitored (and perhaps measured) to verify that planned changes have been achieved?
Have you any examples to show success in this respect?

How are the services provided by staff, other than direct carers, monitored (and perhaps measured) to determine whether the supporting services provided in connection with resident care conform to planned arrangements?

Are residents monitored directly to determine whether their quality of life is being maintained and, whenever possible, improved?

Control of nonconforming product (ISO 9001, clause 8.3)

This clause is applicable to nonconforming services for residents.

Do you have a mandatory procedure for control of nonconforming product?

When a resident fails to respond to treatment as expected, is this documented on prescribed forms?
Have nonconformities occurred in this respect (see the 'Important Note')?
Who has the responsibility and authority to make decisions on future action?

(**Important Note**: The failure of a resident to respond to a drug as expected is not to be regarded as a nonconformity since treatment of residents is not an exact science. However, the failure to give the correct amount of a drug (i.e. the drug has been wrongly prescribed), or carelessness on the part of a carer who is responsible for correct administration of drugs and has failed to do so, is to be regarded as a nonconformity, and recorded as such.)

When supporting services in connection with resident care fail to operate as scheduled, or as planned, are such failures documented on the prescribed forms?
Have nonconformities occurred in this respect (see the 'Important Note')?
Who has the responsibility and authority to make decisions to prevent a recurrence of such failures?

Please show me how any other unsatisfactory services (once identified) are documented on the prescribed forms.

Are all nonconformities followed through as specified on the prescribed forms?

How do you ensure that a nonconforming service that has, allegedly, been corrected is subject to re-verification after correction to demonstrate conformity?

Who has the ultimate responsibility and authority to judge whether the action taken has been appropriate?

Analysis of data (ISO 9001, clause 8.4)

> What data are collected and analysed:
> - to demonstrate the effectiveness of the quality management system?
> - to evaluate how continual improvements can be made in the effectiveness of the quality management system?
>
> How are data analysed to provide information relating to:
> - opportunities for corrective actions?
> - opportunities for preventive actions?
> - resident satisfaction?

Improvement (ISO 9001, clause 8.5)

Continual improvement (ISO 9001, clause 8.5.1)

> How does the care home continually improve the effectiveness of the quality management system?
>
> Does the care home bring about improvements in the effectiveness of the quality management system by means of:
>
> - the quality policy?
> - the quality objectives?
> - internal audits?
> - analysis of data?
> - corrective and preventive actions?
> - management reviews of the quality management system?

Corrective action (ISO 9001, clause 8.5.2)

> One of the mandatory procedures is on corrective action.
> Please may I see it?
>
> How are nonconformities and resident complaints identified?
> How many have been recorded in each category over the last six months?
> Is a log kept for each category?
>
> Who is responsible for determining the cause of any nonconformities and resident complaints?
> Please show me a number of different examples.
>
> Who is responsible for determining the need for action(s) to ensure that nonconformities are put right and resident complaints are addressed promptly?
> Please show me a number of different examples.
>
> Who is responsible for implementing appropriate corrective actions needed in both cases?
> Please show me examples.
>
> Who verifies the corrective actions taken?
> Please show me examples.

Are corrective actions reviewed, say, at management review meetings to ensure that they have been effective?
Please show me evidence of such reviews.

Complaints from residents

Are complainants advised immediately after they have lodged a complaint that they can send their complaint to the Commission for Social Care and Inspection?
How are resident complaints identified?
How many complaints have been recorded over the last six months?
Please may I see a number of complaints, chosen at random?
Is a log kept of all complaints received from residents?

Who is responsible for determining the cause of any resident complaints?
Please show me a number of causes that have been identified.

Who is responsible for determining the need for action(s) to ensure that resident complaints are addressed properly?
Please may I see a few examples to confirm that this is the case?

Who is responsible for implementing corrective actions?
Please show me examples of corrective actions taken.

Who has verified the corrective actions taken?
Please show me examples of verification.

Are corrective actions reviewed, say, at management review meetings to ensure that they have all been effective?
Please show me evidence of such reviews.

Preventive action (ISO 9001, clause 8.5.3)

One of the mandatory procedures is on preventive action.
Please may I see it?

Who is responsible for deciding when there is a need to take preventive action because of a nonconformity?

Who is responsible for deciding when there is a need to take preventive action because of a resident complaint?

Does the care home have a risk management committee?
How often does it meet?
Who is responsible for risk management?
Is there an overall risk management document?
Is the risk management document available to everyone?
Are risk management appraisals carried out and documented?
What routine contingency planning for untoward events has taken place in relation to:

- cross-infection in the care home?
- a health and safety policy?
  - Is there a health and safety document that is applicable to all employees?
  - Who is responsible for health and safety?

- Is there an annual report on health and safety?
- Are all employees trained in health and safety?
- a major incidents plan?
- a fire safety policy?
  - Are fire safety arrangements checked routinely?
- a waste disposal policy?
- disposal of clinical waste?
- security measures?
  - What arrangement exists for the safe-keeping of residents' belongings?
  - How is access to care home buildings controlled?
  - How are staff identified?
  - How are residents protected from physical and verbal abuse?

How are drugs controlled?

Are risk assessments updated in the light of changed circumstances and untoward incidents?

Are untoward incidents, including clinical untoward incidents and near misses, fully documented for discussion at the risk management committee?

Are risk analysis (RA) numbers determined for particular risks?

Who is responsible for deciding when there is a need to take preventive action because of a high RA number, (or a high consequence rating associated with that number) for a particular activity in a care home process?

Have other risk management techniques been used that have resulted in preventive actions being taken?

Can you please show me examples in which preventive actions have been taken?

How does the care home decide who will be responsible for implementing preventive actions?

Please show me examples.

Who verifies the preventive actions taken?

Please show me examples.

Are preventive actions reviewed, say, at management review meetings to ensure that they have been effective?

Please show me evidence of such reviews.

Who is responsible for ensuring that appropriate care home employees are made aware of the importance of preventing untoward events and the documentation that is in place for dealing with such events?

Does the personnel department keep records of all relevant training?

Appendix 1:
Quality management system mandatory procedures

This appendix includes the mandatory procedures for ISO 9001. It is recommended that any other procedures, mandatory or otherwise, follow the same format. The mandatory procedures are as follows.

PC 101   Control of Documents

PC 102   Control of Records

PC 103   Internal Audit

PC 104   Control of Nonconforming Product

PC 105   Corrective Action

PC 106   Preventive Action

Quality Management System Procedure

Control of Documents

Controlled Copy

Copy no: ....

Registered holder: ....

Position: ....

Prepared by: .... Approved by: ....

Management representative

Date: .... Supersedes: ....

PC 101 Issue 1

1.   Purpose

The purpose of this procedure is to show how documents are controlled within the quality management system.

The rigid controls that are imposed on such documents are there for a specific purpose, namely, to ensure that only approved documents, and the latest current issue and the latest revision of documents are in use in all locations throughout the home.

2.   Scope

This procedure applies to all the documents within the quality management system. The framework documentation includes:

>   the quality manual (QM 01);

>   process diagrams (PD 101, etc.);

>   policies (PL 101, etc.);

>   procedures (PC 101, etc.);

>   work instructions (WI 101, etc.)

>   forms (FM 101, etc.);

>   external documents (ED 101 etc.);

>   external forms (EFM 101, etc.).

Working documents (see chapter 4) will include resident care files, nursing care files, and medication documents, amongst others. Personal files such as these should be clearly identified by the name of the resident who resides in the home or who once lived in the home.

Other documents can be created as deemed necessary by the management representative.

3.   Responsibilities

It is the responsibility of the management representative to control all the documentation associated with the quality management system: the framework documents, working documents and records.

4.   Associated documents

Forms:

>   Control of Framework Documentation, FM 101

>   Acceptance of Documentation, FM 102

>   Register of Framework Documentation, FM 103

>   Framework Documentation – Change Request, FM 104

>   Changes to Framework Documentation, FM 105

5.   Details of procedure

5.1   Control of documents

The management representative is responsible for giving final approval to all documents that are part of the home's quality management system.

It is inevitable that some documents will have to be changed from time to time. These must be reapproved by the management representative prior to being reissued to interested parties.

Changes to external documents and external forms cannot be made by the home, but the management representative has the responsibility of ensuring that they are properly controlled.

5.2 Reference letters and numbers, and issue and revision numbers

5.2.1 Reference letters and numbers

The reference letters that precede reference numbers, issue numbers and revision numbers have been allocated as follows:

QM	quality management system policy manual
PD	process diagram
PC	procedure
PT	protocol
WI	work instruction
PL	policies
FM	form
EFM	external form
ED	external document

The appendices to the quality manual provide useful information and stand-alone documents as an important part of the quality manual.

External forms and external documents need to be considered as part of the quality management system documentation since they might have some bearing on the quality of the services provided by the home. Hence they need to be properly controlled.

Each document is given a unique reference number, e.g. 001, which follows the reference letters. In some cases blocks of numbers, e.g. 101 to 150 are allocated to certain departments or certain activities.

5.2.2 Issue and revision numbers

The issue number of a document is indicated by an appendage, 1, 2, 3, etc. An original page does not have a revision status, but if a single page is altered in any way it is given a revision appendage, e.g. Rev. 1, which indicates the first revision status of a page. Further revisions of the same page become Rev. 2, Rev. 3, etc.

When a number of pages have undergone revision, the document can be reissued without revision numbers, but with the grading of Issue 2, Issue 3, etc. The management representative decides when this will be done.

Forms do not have revision numbers, only issue numbers.

External forms and external documents are listed in a logical manner by the management representative.

5.3 Distribution of documents

Each copy of the quality manual or a procedure is given a unique copy number. When controlled documents are despatched to a member of staff they are accompanied by form FM 101. An Acceptance of Documentation form FM 102 will also be sent. This must be signed by the recipient and returned to the management representative.

When, for instance, a procedure is reissued following a number of changes, the superseded documents must be returned to the management representative. Single pages that have been superseded must be destroyed by the recipient of the new pages. Such measures should prevent the continuing use of superseded documents. If the management representative decides to keep superseded documents for 'knowledge preservation purposes' or for any other reasons, they are clearly identified as such by being stamped 'superseded'.

It is the responsibility of the head of a unit or department to ensure that relevant versions of applicable documents are always available at points of use. Such documents must remain legible and be readily identifiable.

The appendices to the quality manual will change from time to time; these will be issued to recipients in a controlled manner.

Documents of external origin are listed by the management representative. They are distributed, and updated when necessary, in the same manner as any other documents. This ensures that only the latest version of any external document, or external form, is being used.

The management representative uses form FM 103 to keep a record of where documents have been sent.

5.4   Changes to documents

All staff are encouraged to make suggestions on how to improve the documents on which the hospital's quality management system is based. Any such changes should first be discussed with immediate colleagues who might be affected by the proposed changes.

Requests for any changes should be made on a Change Request form, FM 104. This is submitted to the management representative who after due consultation with interested parties, and perhaps after discussion in a management review meeting, may issue an amendment to the documentation in accordance with the following steps.

Changes in a document are identified by a vertical line placed in the left hand margin, alongside the changed line(s) or paragraph(s). When a page is changed in this way the revision number is increased as explained above. When a further change is made on the same page only the latest change is indicated by a vertical line.

When a number of changes have been made to a document the management representative may decide to reprint and redistribute the document with a new issue number (with no revision number).

Form FM 105 is also issued to staff along with any changes to the documents. Such forms summarize the changes made to a particular document, including the latest changes. They are intended to be retained as an appendix to the document in question, so that anyone can see at a glance what changes have been made. As appendices, they are placed at the back of the relevant part of the documentation.

5.5   Quality management system forms

A complete set of controlled forms will be held in a designated place accessible within the home. They can be copied for use as and when necessary.

Changes to forms are addressed in the same way as any changes to any other documents.

External documents and external forms are listed in a logical manner by the quality manager.

5.6   Uncontrolled documents

Each controlled document is stamped 'controlled copy' in red ink. Copying of the framework documentation is not normally allowed, with the exception of external documents and external forms, since such uncontrolled copies would defeat the whole objective of maintaining controls on the quality management system documentation. Uncontrolled documents can easily be identified, as the red 'controlled copy' stamp will either be absent or not be red. Nevertheless, occasionally, there may be a need for extra copies of a document to be available, e.g. for discussion purposes at a meeting. If such a need arises, copies may be made with the approval of the management representative, but each copy should be clearly stamped: 'uncontrolled'. The uncontrolled copies should be withdrawn from circulation as soon as practicable.

In the case of uncontrolled copies that are issued in formulating a quality plan, the uncontrolled copies may become an integrated part of the quality plan and as such will need to remain in situ perhaps for some considerable time, if the quality plan becomes dormant. However, when such a quality plan is reactivated, the project manager will obtain from the management representative a controlled copy of the relevant document and the uncontrolled copy will be returned.

5.7   Documents (and records) on computer

Many documents and records (see PC 102) are stored on computer. The same rules apply to electronic storage as apply to storage of hard copy documents and records, but additional safeguards are required in the way of back-up storage, prevention of unauthorized access to data, as well as prevention of corruption of data, etc.

The management representative has to be satisfied that adequate controls are in place for these purposes.

5.8   Bureaucratic documentation

The quality management system documentation must not be bureaucratic. If any member of staff believes that a document serves little or no useful purpose, such thoughts should be aired with colleagues with a view to getting the bureaucratic document amended or removed from the quality management system via the management representative.

Control of Framework Documentation

To: _____

Listed below, and attached hereto, are controlled documents for your retention. Please ensure that the documents are accessible to your colleagues so that there can be no misunderstanding as to how the home functions.

_____

_____

_____

_____

_____

_____

_____

_____

_____

_____

_____

_____

I shall be glad to receive any suggestions for improving the documentation.

If you are receiving a document which supersedes an existing one, please ensure that you return the superseded document at the same time.

Date: _____

Management representative: _____

FM 101   Issue 1.

Acceptance of Documentation

To: the management representative

I accept the safe receipt of the following controlled documents:

....

....

....

....

....

I am returning the following superseded documents:

....

....

....

....

....

I shall be glad to receive any suggestions for improving the documentation.

If you are receiving a document which supersedes an existing one, please ensure that you return the supersede document at the same time.

Date: ....

Recipient: ....

FM 102   Issue 1.

Register of Framework Documentation

Reference no.	Issued to	Date issued	Signature of management representative

FM 103   Issue 1.

Page of

Framework Documentation – Change Request

Reference:

Proposed change:

Requested by: .... Date: ....

Position: .... Department: ....

Comments sought from:

Comments by reviewer(s):

Signature(s) of reviewer(s): ....

Date: ....

Approved/rejected
by management representative: .... Date: ....

FM 104 Issue 1.

Changes to Framework Documentation

Reference no.	Amendment/additions	Date issued	Signature of management representative

FM 105   Issue 1.   Page   of

Quality Management System Procedure

Control of Records

Controlled Copy

Copy no: ....

Registered holder: ....

Position: ....

Prepared by: .... Approved by: ....

Management representative

Date: .... Supersedes: ....

PC 102 Issue 1

1. Purpose

The purpose of this procedure is to ensure that records are established and maintained so as to prove that the quality management system is in place; that it is working effectively in accordance with the home's quality policy; and in pursuance of the home's policy of maintaining and, whenever possible, improving the quality of life of all the residents.

2. Scope

This procedure applies to all the documents specified in ISO 9001 as well as many working document records such as those associated with care plans, medication, etc. The management representative might wish to add other records in the light of experience.

3. Responsibilities

The management representative is responsible for ensuring that records are collected, suitably filed and stored, etc. Responsibility for records in the first instance lies with carers who create and use the records. All staff are expected to contribute directly, or indirectly, towards the establishment and maintenance of records during their everyday activities.

4. Associated documents

These are too diverse to list individually, since records arise from many quality management system documents and from day-to-day operations.

5. Details of procedure

5.1 Quality records

Records arise from the many activities that occur in the home. They provide objective evidence as to what has happened.

ISO 9001 requires, as a minimum, certain listed records to be kept and maintained. They provide objective evidence as to what has occurred. These are records on the following:

(a) management review meetings (see clause 5.6.1);

(b) education, training, skills and experience (see clause 6.2.2);

(c) evidence that realization processes and their results meet planned arrangements, i.e. the home will establish and maintain day-to-day resident records that will help demonstrate that it is maintaining and, where possible, improving the quality of life of residents (see clause 7.1);

(d) results from the evaluation of suppliers and the necessary actions arising from the evaluations, if applicable (see clause 7.4.1);

(e) validation of processes where the resulting output cannot be verified by subsequent monitoring or measurement, e.g. use of sterilizers (see clause 7.5.2);

(f) results of any calibrations on equipment, if applicable (see clause 7.6);

(g) validity of any previous measurements when measuring equipment is found to be, or suspected of being, out of calibration (see clause 7.6);

(h) results of internal audits and actions arising thereafter (see clause 8.2.2);

(i) nonconformities (see clause 8.3);

(j) corrective actions and their signing off (see clause 8.5.2);

(k)   resident complaints and their outcomes (see clause 8.5.2);

(l)   preventive actions and their effectiveness (see clause 8.5.3).

In addition, a home should establish and maintain records on:

(m)   changes to the quality management system's documentation (see PC 101);

(n)   documentation relating to assessments, surveillances, etc. by a certification body;

(o)   monitoring of resident satisfaction;

(p)   contracts;

(q)   maintenance carried out within the home that might have a bearing on the quality of resident care, e.g. temperature control of water;

(r)   quality plans and other documents that are considered relevant to the care of residents;

(s)   review of quality objectives (see clause 5.4.1);

(t)   review of quality policy (as and when deemed necessary) (see clause 5.3);

(u)   any other records that management deem should be kept for regulatory and statutory reasons and/or for continuing quality care of residents.

5.2   Collection, care and collation of records

Everyone associated with the creation of records must ensure that they are readily identified; are legible and remain legible; are stored appropriately; are protected from damage; and can be easily retrieved.

The management representative is responsible for the collection and collation of records arising directly from the quality management system documents. They also have to be satisfied that staff are collecting and collating their records in a satisfactory manner.

Storage will initially take place in designated areas following discussion with appropriate staff. Longer-term storage will also be decided in consultation with the management representative.

Once each year the management representative has to confirm in writing to the management review committee that all the defined records are in place, properly filed, preserved, etc.

Many records are stored on computer. The same rules apply to electronic storage as apply to storage of hard copy records, but additional safeguards are required in the way of back-up storage, prevention of unauthorized access to data, prevention of corruption of data, etc. (see procedure PC 101).

5.3   Filing of quality records

All records are filed appropriately and securely.

5.4   Access to records

Access to records will be restricted to senior staff only and those who need to have access because of their day-to-day responsibilities. Any resident has the right to examine their own records.

5.5   Maintenance of records

The management representative is responsible for maintaining the records directly associated with the quality management system. Likewise, other staff who have responsibilities for initiating records based on their day-to-day activities are also responsible for their upkeep.

5.6   Archiving of records

All records will be archived from time to time by the management representative in a manner that will allow easy traceability and retrieval when required. Records are kept and maintained in a sound condition for a minimum period of years, decided by the home, except in those cases in which records are required by law to be maintained for specific periods of time.

5.7   Disposal of quality records

Only the chief executive, or some other nominated person, in consultation with the management representative, can give approval for the disposal of records after the stated retention times have been exceeded. Accounting records are retained for at least seven years, but all other records are usually disposed of after the specified times.

Quality Management System Procedure

Internal Audit

Controlled Copy

Copy no: ....

Registered holder: ....

Position: ....

Prepared by: .... Approved by: ....

Management representative

Date: .... Supersedes: ....

PC 103 Issue 1

1.   Purpose

The purpose of this procedure is to explain how internal audits are conducted on all aspects of the home's quality management system with a view to establishing that the:

quality management system complies with the requirements of ISO 9001;

quality management system is being effectively implemented and maintained;

quality management system conforms to the planned arrangements so that the quality of life of each resident is being maintained and, where possible, improved.

The internal audits must be conducted at planned intervals and are intended to highlight any problems or difficulties and afford opportunities to make approved changes.

2.   Scope

This procedure applies to all the internal auditing activities that are undertaken by or on behalf of the home.

3.   Responsibilities

It is the responsibility of the management representative, or a person nominated by the owner of the home, or the registered person to ensure that internal auditing is being done satisfactorily.

4.   Associated documents

Quality management system manual.

Forms:

Internal Audit Schedule, FM 121;

Register of Internal Audits, FM 122;

Internal Audit Questionnaire, FM 123;

Nonconformity or Observation Form, FM 124;

Summary – Internal Audit Report, FM 125.

5.   Details of procedure

5.1   General

Internal auditing is one of the most important aspects of the home's quality management system. It must be viewed in a positive manner, because internal quality auditing affords an opportunity to all parties involved to consider ways of improving how the home functions for the benefit of residents.

5.2   Auditors

All auditing will be conducted by auditors who have received appropriate training. No auditor is allowed to audit their own work, but auditors can audit work for which they are responsible. Thus, a care manager can audit the work of the senior carers and the carers allocated to them, but a care manager cannot audit the actual work that he or she does. This could be done by, say, the registered person for the home or by one of the more experienced senior carers.

5.3 Planning of internal audits

The management representative ensures that there is a comprehensive schedule for internal auditing at planned intervals, which embraces all aspects of work carried out in the home. Some areas of work that are key to the home's activities may undergo internal auditing at frequent intervals. In addition, when an audit identifies problems, re-auditing will be arranged in the near future on an agreed date.

The overall schedule for internal audits throughout the home is available for all members of staff to examine.

During the implementation of the quality management system, internal quality audits can be carried out as soon as an activity is considered to be ready for an audit. Proper records of findings are made of all audits, including the preliminary ones.

An internal audit schedule can be prepared on form FM 121. This schedule will show the dates on which internal audits will be conducted in different areas of the home. The form will identify processes and/or activities to be audited and the corresponding relevant areas of the standard.

Audits can be delayed or postponed in exceptional circumstances, but only with the approval of the owner, or the registered person and the management representative. Additional audits will be arranged by the management representative in consultation with others when a previous audit has proved to be unsatisfactory.

5.4 Internal audit register

Prior to any audit, the management representative will allocate a number to an audit and record the actual date of it on the Register of Internal Audits, FM 122. All subsequent documents associated with the particular audit will include the audit number and date.

The management representative is responsible for maintaining the register at all times so that the status of internal audits can be readily determined at any time.

5.5 Audit questions

Prior to any audit, an auditor will prepare a number of possible questions (Internal Audit Questionnaire, FM 123) in connection with the area being audited. These will form the basis of the audit, but other questions may be asked in the light of what is subsequently revealed to an auditor.

It has been made clear to all members of staff that any member of staff may be asked questions by an auditor in order for them to determine whether the quality management system documentation (a process, procedure, or work instruction, etc.) is being implemented satisfactorily and whether it is effective.

5.6 Findings of internal audits

Whenever an auditor discovers that there is a discrepancy (against the requirements of the standard, a process, procedure, or work instruction, etc.) between what is laid down and what is actually taking place in the home, objective evidence to this effect will be recorded on a Nonconformity or Observation Form, FM 124. The auditee will be asked to sign the form, thus indicating their agreement with the findings.

At the end of the audit this form is sent to the management representative after corrective and preventive actions have been addressed.

5.7   Corrective action

The Nonconformity or Observation Form, FM 124, will need other entries. Someone, for instance, will have to state on the forms what action is to be taken. On occasions this may have to be completed after an audit; the person responsible for such action has to be named and their signature obtained. Observations might not result in the need for action to be taken. The date by which any changes are to be implemented also has to be given (see procedure PC 105).

5.8   Preventive action

If preventive action is to be taken, it must be entered on the Nonconformity or Observation Form, FM 124. The person responsible for such action has to be named and their signature obtained. The date by which the changes are to be implemented also has to be given (see procedure PC 106).

5.9   Verification of corrective and preventive action

It is the responsibility of the management representative to add their signature to the form once verification of the corrective action, and possibly preventive action, has been confirmed.

5.10   Summary of internal audit

The auditor will complete a summary – an Internal Audit Report (FM 125) – after each audit where the main findings (nonconformities and observations) are recorded along with an overall summary of the audit.

At the end of the audit all the forms are sent to the management representative.

5.11   Completion of register of internal audits

Following completion of an internal audit, the management representative will enter the relevant information in the Register of Internal Audits, FM 122. If no nonconformities or observations have been found the 'audit completed' section can be signed off immediately, otherwise, the audit will be signed off only when the management representative is satisfied that the points raised have been completed satisfactorily.

5.12   Management reviews

The internal audit reports are considered at each management review meeting. They are used as the basis for any discussions on the successful implementation of the home's quality management system.

The management review committee has the authority to introduce changes via the management representative with a view to continual improvement of the effectiveness of the quality management system.

5.13   Quality records

All the documents associated with internal audits will form part of the home's quality records. These will be retained for a minimum period specified by the registered person.

Nonconformity or Observation Forms (FM 124) will all be filed consecutively eventually, but as an interim measure all outstanding Nonconformity or Observation Forms will be filed together in two groups. As each outstanding corrective action (and possibly preventive action) is signed off by the management representative the form will be transferred to its appropriate sequential position in the 'closed-off' section of the file.

Internal Audit Schedule, 2006

	Jan	Feb	Mar	Apr	May	June	July	Aug	Sept	Oct	Nov	Dec
Planned month Actual month												
Planned date Actual date												
Process/activity Reference process diagrams and/or Name of the relevant clause ISO 9001 clause no.												

Date: _____   Signature of management representative: _____

FM 121 Issue 1.

Register of internal audits

Audit no.	Date of audit	Activity reference document(s)	Completion date for corrective action(s)	Completion date for preventative action(s)	Signature of management representative following verification

Page   of

Internal Audit Questionnaire

Audit no: _____

Process/activity/reference documents: _____

Manual, process, procedure, form	ISO 9001 reference	Question	Comments

Page   of

FM 123   Issue 1.

Nonconformity or Observation Form

Audit no: ....   Nonconformity or Observation no: ....

Process/activity	Reference documents	Date

Nonconformity or observation (as appropriate):

Auditor: ....   Signature: ....

Departmental representative: ....   Signature: ....

Nonconformity – Corrective action(s) proposed or observation – Resulting in continual improvements:

Person responsible for corrective
action(s) or improvements: ....   Signature: ....

Date by which corrective action(s) or improvements will be implemented: ....

Preventive action(s) proposed (write N/A if no preventive action is proposed):

Person responsible for
preventive action(s): ....   Signature: ....

Date by which preventive action(s) will be implemented: ....

Verification of corrective action(s) and preventive action(s)/adoption or rejection of observation

Signature of management
representative: ....   Date: ....

FM 124 Issue 1.   Page   of

114

Summary – Internal Audit Report

Audit no: _____ Nonconformity or Observation no:_____

Process/activity	Reference documents	Date

Nonconformity:

Observations:

Overall summary:

Auditor (print name):_____ Signature:_____

Quality Management System Procedure

Control of Nonconforming Product

Controlled Copy

Copy no: ....

Registered holder: ....

Position: ....

Prepared by: .... Approved by: ....

Management representative

Date: .... Supersedes: ....

PC 104 Issue 1

1. Purpose

The purpose of this procedure is to ensure that all nonconformities are properly documented and followed through by corrective action(s) and possibly preventive action(s).

Nonconformities can arise from a number of sources:

the failure to follow agreed processes;

the failure to follow agreed procedures, work instructions, etc;

during internal audits;

as a result of complaints from residents or their relatives and friends.

2. Scope

This procedure applies to all nonconformities.

3. Responsibilities

It is the responsibility of the management representative to ensure that all nonconformities are dealt with in the manner prescribed in this procedure.

4. Associated documents

Forms:

Register of Internal Audits Form, FM 122 (see PC 103, Internal Audit)

Nonconformity or Observation Form, FM 124 (see PC 103, Internal Audit)

Register of Nonconformities (Independent of Internal Audits), FM 131

Nonconformity Form (Independent of Internal Audits), FM 132

Register of Complaints, FM 141 (see PC 105, Corrective Action)

Complaint Form, FM 142 (see PC 105, Corrective Action)

5. Details of procedure

5.1 Nonconformities

All nonconformities found in the home must be properly recorded. The nature of the nonconformity and the name of the person who caused the nonconformity, if this is known, are clearly recorded on the Nonconformity or Observation Form, FM 124 or Nonconformity form, FM 132. In some cases, of course, the cause of nonconformity may not be the result of any individual's action, or inaction.

Any nonconformity in relation to the quality of care of residents must be addressed with minimum delay. A record must be kept of the corrective action taken on the nonconformity form. The management representative must be kept fully informed. Only when the management representative, or some such person, is satisfied that the nonconformity has been dealt with satisfactorily will the form be signed off. It is retained as a record (see PC 102).

A complaint from a resident might have arisen because of a nonconformity (See PC 105). In such cases forms FM 141 and FM 142 should be used.

The effects of the corrective action taken for the benefit of a resident must be subject to discussion with the resident to ensure that the action taken has been effective.

All other nonconformities, whatever their source, are addressed in the same manner, except that some might not require an immediate response in the way of corrective actions.

5.2   Review of causes of nonconformities

Nonconformities will arise for many reasons in any organization: human failure, incompetence, disregard for procedures or other documentation, or an impractical procedure or process, etc. which has not been properly tried and tested before its introduction.

All factual information on nonconformities must be reviewed immediately following their discovery to ascertain the cause of nonconformities and to decide whether immediate corrective action is required.

In some cases when a nonconformity becomes known, the registered person must decide whether the same nonconformity might have occurred previously with a number of other residents.

5.3   Prevention of repetition of nonconformity

It is important to ensure that there is not a repetition of a nonconformity. The third part of the appropriate Nonconformity Form or Complaint Form will be completed, if possible, perhaps after discussion with the other interested parties, to prevent a recurrence of the nonconformity in the future (see PC 106).

In those cases in which a single human failing has caused the nonconformity 'N/A' (not applicable) can be written in this section.

5.4   Verification of any corrective actions and any further actions

The Nonconformity Form is handed to the management representative as soon as possible.

The management representative will then sign the last section of the form once they are satisfied that any corrective actions and any preventive actions have been carried out satisfactorily and that the final outcome has been satisfactory.

5.5   Register of nonconformities

The management representative is responsible for maintaining the appropriate register of all nonconformities.

5.6   Filing of nonconformities

A file will be maintained for nonconformities. The file will be divided into two parts: the first part will contain 'active' nonconformities, and the second will contain those that are 'closed'.

5.7   Management review meetings

The management representative will regularly review all factual information on nonconformities and present at the next management review meeting their findings on all the different kinds of nonconformities that have been recorded since the last meeting. The regular management review meetings will provide an opportunity for wider discussions of any nonconformities. Unplanned management review meetings can, of course, be called at any time. Nonconformities based on customer complaints will require action immediately a suspected nonconformity arises.

The meeting will consider what action to take about those reported at the last meeting that still have to be signed off or closed.

The registered person will be in a better position to manage the home if:

- nonconformities are identified;

- the reasons for the nonconformities are identified;

- appropriate corrective and perhaps preventive actions are taken;

- the documentation of the nonconformity and subsequent action(s) are complete.

5.8   Quality records

All the documentation associated with nonconformities will form part of the home's quality records.

Records on nonconformities will be maintained for a minimum period of time as specified by the registered person.

Register of Nonconformities

No.	Nonconformity	Date discovered	Signature of management representative following corrective/preventive action

FM 131   Issue 1.   Page   of

Nonconformity Form

No: ....

Resident: ....

Telephone no: ....

Reference no: .... Internal ref. no: ....

Nature of nonconformity:

Signature: .... Date discovered: ....

Corrective action(s) taken:

Person responsible
for corrective action(s): ....

Date: .... Signature: ....

Preventive action(s) proposed:

Person responsible
for preventive action(s): .... Signature: ....

Date by which preventive action(s) will be implemented: ....

Verification of corrective action(s) and preventive action(s)

Signature of management
representative: .... Date: ....

FM 132 Issue 1.

Quality Management System Procedure

Corrective Action
(Arising from Nonconformities and Customers' Complaints)

Controlled Copy

Copy no: ....

Registered holder: ....

Position: ....

Prepared by: .... Approved by: ....

Management representative

Date: .... Supersedes: ....

PC 105 Issue 1

1.   Purpose

The purpose of this procedure is to ensure that corrective action is taken to eliminate the cause of any nonconformity in order to correct what is going wrong or what has gone wrong. This procedure also applies when corrective action is taken in response to any nonconformities, however discovered, and when complaints are received from residents or their representatives.

Corrective actions must always be appropriate to the impact of the problems encountered and the likelihood of it happening again. For example, a vast amount of money should not be spent after a single nonconformity or a single complaint when either is considered to be a one-off event with a very low probability of happening again.

On the other hand if it is thought that the same, or similar, nonconformity or resident complaint might reoccur, additional action, known as preventive action, might be taken to ensure that this is not the case. Sometimes, such preventive action might become part of the corrective action, if the action taken is greater than the essential corrective action necessary to put right what was going wrong or had gone wrong. In general it is better to think of corrective actions and preventive action as being quite distinct and separate.

Sometimes corrective actions might require immediate attention because nonconformity in a residential home may have serious consequences if not dealt with immediately, and resident complaints, even apparently trivial complaints, must be addressed without delay.

Preventive actions should be implemented as soon as possible (see procedure PC 106, Preventive Action).

2.   Scope

This procedure applies to all nonconformities whether they are identified by a member of staff in the home or by a third party. It also applies to complaints received from residents or their family and friends.

3.   Responsibilities

It is the responsibility of the management representative to ensure that all corrective actions are dealt with in an expeditious manner and that appropriate documentation is raised.

4.   Associated documents

Process diagrams:

Residents' complaints, PD 104

Forms:

Nonconformity or Observation Form, FM 124 (see PC 103)

Register of Nonconformities, FM 131 (see PC 104)

Nonconformity, FM 132 (see PC 104)

Register of Complaints, FM 141

Complaint Form, FM 142

5.   Details of procedure

5.1   Corrective action in response to nonconformities

Corrective action is essentially a backwards looking phenomenon starting, at the latest, from the time a decision is made that corrective action is necessary in order to put right what is going wrong or what has gone wrong. The implementation of the corrective action may not always be possible immediately, but it will take place as soon as possible or as appropriate in the immediate future.

Once a nonconformity has been identified it is recorded on a prescribed form as explained in procedures PC 103, PC 104 and this procedure.

The person who accepts responsibility for the corrective action must sign the form.

All the forms referred to above include space for preventive action (see procedures PC 103, PC 104 and this procedure).

Finally, the prescribed form should only be signed off by a responsible person within the home, usually the management representative, when they are certain that the nonconformity has been satisfactorily dealt with from every point of view and the actions taken have been completed in every respect.

The corrective action taken should also subsequently be reviewed to decide whether it has been effective in dealing with the nonconformity.

5.2   Complaints by residents (PD 104: Regulation 22, Standard 16))

There should be no doubt as to what is meant by a resident complaint. If anyone in the home feels that it is necessary to apologize to a resident, because they appear to be aggrieved by what has happened or, maybe, by what has not happened, then a complaint has been received. It may appear to be an unjustifiable complaint, but if the resident evidently thinks otherwise it would be wise to tread cautiously and to promise to investigate the complaint without undue delay.

Process diagram, PD 104, outlines the suggested steps to be followed by the registered person when a complaint is received from a resident. All residents should have been told on taking up residence that all complaints can be submitted to the Commission for Social Care and Inspection (CSCI). The resident is reminded of this whenever a complaint is made and the address and telephone number is given to them again when a complaint is made in case they wish to pursue that path.

There are two important points in connection with complaints from residents. First the complaint must be addressed quickly and if it appears to be a serious complaint, it should be referred without delay to the registered person immediately for urgent action. It should also be made clear to a complainant that the complaint made will be addressed as quickly as possible and certainly within 28 days from the time that the complaint was received.

5.3   Corrective action in response to complaints

A Complaint Form, FM 142, similar to the forms FM 124 and FM 132, is used to deal with every complaint. Every complaint must be recorded on the prescribed form, be it a verbal complaint, a complaint made by telephone, by fax, by email or by letter. The form identifies the person who has complained; the date and time of its receipt; the recipient of the complaint; and the nature of the complaint. The form includes space to state the 'corrective action' taken. The person who accepts responsibility for the corrective action must sign that part of the form.

The form includes space for 'preventive action' (see procedure PC 106).

The management representative will sign the last section of the form once the complaint process has been completed.

The management representative is responsible for maintaining the Register of Complaints Form 141, as is the case for the Register of Nonconformities and, similarly, all Complaint Forms (FM 141 and 142) are systematically filed like Nonconformity forms (see procedures PC 103 and 104).

5.4 Management review meetings

The management representative will present at each management review meeting details of all nonconformities and customer complaints, and the home's responses.

Such meetings will consider what action to take about those nonconformities that were reported at the last meeting which still have to be signed off.

All complaints should have been addressed promptly. Management should look upon resident complaints in a positive manner. They are not be used to ostracize people, although when incompetence has become evident, appropriate action needs to be taken by the registered person.

Most residents usually accept with good grace most mistakes, provided corrective action is taken promptly. From the home's point of view, resident goodwill is thereby usually retained, adverse publicity is avoided and litigation is less likely.

5.5 Quality records

All the documentation associated with corrective actions taken in connection with nonconformities and customer complaints form part of the home's quality records.

Register of Complaints

No.	Complaint	Date complaint made	Date and signature of management representative following verification

Complaint Form

No: ....

Organization: ....

Complaint: .... Telephone no: ....

Nature of complaint:

Signature: .... Date : ....

Corrective action(s) taken: Justified/unjustified

Person responsible
for corrective action(s): ....

Date: .... Signature : ....

Preventive action(s) proposed (if any):

Person responsible
for preventive action(s): .... Signature: ....

Date by which preventive action(s) will be implemented: ....

Verification of corrective action(s) and preventive action(s)

Signature of management
representative: .... Date: ....

FM 142 Issue 1.

Quality Management System Procedure

Preventive Action
(arising from Nonconformities,
Customers' Complaints and Risk Management)

Controlled Copy

Copy no: ....

Registered holder: ....

Position: ....

Prepared by: .... Approved by: ....

Management representative

Date: .... Supersedes: ....

PC 106 Issue 1

1.   Purpose

The purpose of this procedure is to ensure that preventive action is taken:

(i)   to reduce the likelihood of an earlier, or a similar nonconformity recurring in the future;

(ii)   to reduce the likelihood of an earlier, or a similar kind of resident complaint recurring in the future;

(iii)   to prevent an untoward event from occurring for the first time, as determined by Risk Assessments (RAs) or Failure Mode and Effect Analyses (FMEAs), etc;

(iv)   to prevent an untoward event from occurring for the first time because of a very high consequence rating for a specific possible fault or mistake;

(v)   to prevent an untoward even from occurring for the first time because of new knowledge, new technology, new evidence, etc.

Preventive action must always be appropriate to the impact of the problem encountered and the likelihood of it happening again. In the second group of possibilities, (iii) to (v), in which an event has not yet occurred, any preventive action taken must likewise be commensurate with the perceived likelihood of the untoward incident taking place, but also with the seriousness of the consequences that might occur.

2.   Scope

This procedure applies to all kinds of preventive actions taken by the home.

3.   Responsibilities

It is the responsibility of the management representative to ensure that all preventive actions are dealt with in an expeditious manner and that appropriate documentation is raised.

4.   Associated documents

Procedures

        PC 103   Internal Audit

        PC 104   Control of Nonconforming Product

        PC 105   Corrective Action (arising from Nonconformities and Complaints)

Forms:

        Nonconformity or Observation Form, FM 124

        Nonconformity Form, FM 132

        Complaint Form, FM 142

5.   Details of procedure

5.1   Preventive actions

Preventive action is essentially a forwards looking phenomenon starting, at the earliest, from the time a decision is made that corrective action is necessary to put right that which is going wrong or has gone wrong. Action, preventive action, might then be taken to prevent a recurrence of a nonconformity or a resident complaint.

Preventive action is also taken to prevent an untoward event from occurring for the first time.

Such preventive action might be considered necessary in the light of risk assessments and the seriousness of the consequences identified in such risk assessments, as well as any new evidence, new knowledge, new technology, etc. that have led the home to believe that an untoward event might happen in the future.

The implementation of the preventive action may not always be possible immediately, but it should take place as soon as possible or practical.

5.2 Nonconformities and customer complaints

5.2.1 Preventive actions and nonconformities

If a decision is taken that there is a need to take preventive action this should be entered on the Nonconformity or Observation Form, FM 124 (see procedures PC 103, Internal Audit), or on form FM 132 (see PC 104, Control of Nonconforming Product). The entry should give the name of the individual responsible for carrying out the preventive action and the date by which it is to be completed.

Sometimes preventive action is necessary because of one incident in which the outcome was of serious consequence, or might have been of serious consequence. The case for preventive action becomes even stronger when similar incidents have occurred before.

5.2.2 Preventive actions and customer complaints

Sometimes preventive action is necessary because of one complaint in which the outcome was of serious consequence to a resident, or might have been. If a decision is taken that there is a need to take preventive action this should be entered on the Complaint Form, FM 142 (see PC 105, Corrective Action).

Sometimes preventive action might be necessary because of several similar complaints, as explained in the previous section. The case for taking preventive action becomes even stronger when similar complaints have occurred before.

The entry on form FM 142 should give the name of the individual responsible for carrying out the preventive action and the date by which it is to be completed.

5.2.3 Verification of any preventive actions arising from nonconformities and complaints

In the case of preventive actions arising from nonconformities and resident complaints, the prescribed forms (FM 124, FM 132 and FM 142) should only be signed off by a responsible person within the organization, usually the management representative, when they are satisfied that any proposed preventive actions have been implemented. The preventive actions must also be reviewed to verify that the action taken has been effective in dealing with the nonconformity or resident complaint.

5.3 Prevention of future untoward events

5.3.1 Routine planning

Resident safety in homes is of paramount importance. Yet there are risks to be faced by many residents in homes. For instance, there are potential risks from cross-infections simply by being in a home or visiting one. Such risks are nothing compared with the risks incurred by all of us when outside homes, i.e. road accidents. Nevertheless, the registered person in a home will have documentation in place to minimize the risks involved in a number of areas. These will include the health and safety policy, fire safety policy and documentation relating to cross-infection in the home.

Such documentation includes standard procedures and actions that should prevent any untoward events or, at worst, minimize the effects of untoward events involving residents and staff in the home.

The management representative is responsible for ensuring that all such documentation is kept up to date in accordance with the latest statutory and legal requirements.

The management representative is responsible for ensuring that all employees are regularly briefed on the prevention of untoward events and on the documents that are in place for dealing with such events. The registered person will ensure that records are kept on all staff who attend briefings on possible untoward events.

5.3.2 Risk Assessments (RAs): Risk Analysis Numbers

When contemplating future untoward events, it is helpful to make an estimate of the likelihood of an untoward event happening and the resulting consequences should it happen.

Simple risk analysis is a method of combining both the likelihood and consequences of an untoward event. The Risk Analysis Number is based on two estimated numbers.

Risk Analysis Number = qualitative measure of probability of an untoward event occurring
qualitative measure of the consequences of its occurrence

A qualitative measure of the **probability** of an untoward event occurring can be rated between 1 and 10 as follows:

1. Impossible.

2. Rare. Event will occur only in exceptional circumstances.

4. Unlikely. The event could occur sometime.

6. Moderate. The event will occur at some time.

8. Likely. The event will occur.

10. Certain. The event is expected to occur sometime.

A qualitative measure of the **consequence** of an untoward event occurring might be rated between 1 and 10 as follows:

1. Negligible. No injuries. No financial loss.

2. Minor. First aid treatment. Moderate financial loss.

4. Serious. Medical treatment necessary. High financial implications, etc.

6. Major. Excessive injuries. Major financial loss, etc.

8. Single death.

10. Multiple deaths.

Qualitative risk assessment matrix

Probability	Impossible	Rare	Unlikely	Moderate	Likely	Certain
	1	2	4	6	8	10
Consequence						
Negligible	1	1	2	4	6	8	10
Minor	2	2	4	8	12	16	20
Serious	4	4	8	16	24	32	40
Major	6	6	12	24	36	48	**60**
Death	8	8	16	32	48	**64**	**80**
Deaths	10	10	20	40	**60**	**80**	**100**

The two numbers chosen are multiplied together to give a Risk Analysis (RA) number. The levels of Risk Matrix can be established using all possible combinations of numbers. Each number provides an estimate of the probability of an untoward event happening. The higher the number, the more serious the failure mode. The chart clearly indicates that an untoward event has virtually 'no risk' at one extreme and 'high risk' at the other, as shown by the **bold** numbers 60, 64, 80 and 100.

In cases of calculated high risk for an event happening, then preventive action, or actions, are taken to reduce the probability of an untoward event occurring. The high risk numbers should help an organization to get is priorities right in deciding what preventive actions (not corrective actions) should be addressed.

5.3.3 High consequence rating

Although the calculated RA numbers are extremely useful, preventive action, or actions, are also given to any possible causes of failure that have been given a high consequence rating such as 8 and 10.

5.3.4 Other risk management techniques

Other risk management techniques are available for enthusiasts in risk management. One such technique is known as Failure Mode and Effective Analysis (FMEA). This is a little more sophisticated than the simple technique referred to above and is based on three estimated numbers, not two.

5.3.5 New evidence, new knowledge, etc.

Sometimes new evidence comes to light, new knowledge or the availability of new technology, etc., that suggests that preventive action should be taken to prevent what hitherto was not considered to be a likelihood of an untoward event occurring.

5.4 Records

All changes arising from preventive actions will be recorded and maintained for future reference.

Appendix 2:
References

Standards publications

ISO 9001:2000, *Quality Management Systems – Requirements*

Other publications

[1]   National Care Standards Commission. *The Management of Medication in Care Services, 2002–2003.* The Stationery Office (TSO) Ltd, 2004. ISBN 0 11 703379 0.

[2]   'Care Homes Probe' in *Which?* Issue April 2004, p. 6. Hertford: The Consumers Association.

[3]   *The Care Homes Regulations, 2001.* The Stationery Office (TSO) Ltd, 2001. ISBN 0 11 039231 0.

[4]   Department of Health. *Care Homes for Older People: National Minimum Standards, 2003.* The Stationery Office (TSO) Ltd, 2003. ISBN 0 11 322579 2.

[5]   Green, D. *ISO 9000 Quality Systems Auditing.* Gower Publications Ltd, Aldershot, 1997. ISBN 0 5660 7900 3.

[6]   ISO 9000 and ISO 14001 certificates, 13th Survey (for 2003). Data can be obtained from any ISO member and from ISO Central Secretariat. ISBN 0 5660 7900 3 (http://www.iso.ch).

[7]   The Royal Pharmaceutical Society of Great Britain (RPSGB). *The Administration and Control of Medicines in Care Homes and Children's Services.* Published by RPSGB, London: June 2003.